Intellectual
Foundations of China

STUDIES IN WORLD CIVILIZATION

Intellectual Foundations of China

Frederick W. Mote
Princeton University

 Alfred A. Knopf, New York

Second Edition

987654321

Copyright © 1971, 1989 by Alfred A. Knopf, Inc.

Library of Congress Cataloging-in-Publication Data

    Mote, Frederick W., 1922–
        Intellectual foundations of China / Frederick W. Mote.—[2nd
   ed.]
           p. cm.—(Studies in world civilization)

        Bibliography: p.
        Includes index.
        ISBN 0-394-38338-9
      1. China—Intellectual life. I. Title. II. Series.
    DS721.M73 1989
    931—dc19   88–560
                                         CIP

Cover & Book Design by Sandra Josephson

Manufactured in the United States of America

Preface

What in China's long history explains its special character and its unmatched duration as a living civilization? Of what importance is its past today? In seeking answers to these questions we turn here to the emergence of Chinese intellectual thought in what seems a very remote past. Nonetheless, we propose this idea: The intellectual foundations, laid down then for the civilization which was to stand on them so firmly and so long, must be understood if we want to understand China.

Starting out by assessing the intellectual foundations of a civilization seems particularly appropriate to the study of traditional China. For China's intellectual life was not as highly compartmentalized into separate and sometimes competing categories like philosophy, religion, and science as were most others. Its politics, for example, was the extension of its ethics from the individual to his or her society; its knowledge implied action. China's early thinkers debated vigorously among themselves about all the things that it was useful for people to know, and to do. In the Golden Age of Chinese philosophy, with which historical period this small book is concerned, it is quite possible to seek out the interaction between intellectual thought and the larger culture, particularly in the social and political realms, and to regard that thread of interaction as the most interesting and illuminating one to follow.

Because that thread has remained unbroken and central to Chinese life from those early times to our own, its beginnings are remarkably pertinent to the life of China in our time. Even China's most recent modernizing leaders have attested to that. Both the apparently moribund and the obviously vital aspects of old China's civilization remain relevant to an understanding of China as it is now. Mao Tse-tung and Chiang Kai-shek both acquired their basic literacy through the study of texts in a language that still is a living written style of Chinese, but written well over two thousand years ago. The leaders of no other nation in our century have so directly inherited the mantle—or is it the pall?—of so ancient a cultural past, whether as proponents of its values or as rebels against them, or as both.

This small volume is of course no general history even of the few preimperial centuries with which it is concerned. It is a highly selective discussion of some features of Chinese civilization, stressing the main outlines of intellectual life, because the ideas and the texts conveying them have remained central to all that has followed. It does not attempt to analyze the ideas as pure philosophical concepts in isolation, but to view them as intellectual elements in the larger culture. It represents one historian's retrospective view of the Chinese civilization that has been so imposing a spectacle throughout history, seeking in its formative stages those things which have remained the most important. The ideas that emerged twenty-five hundred years ago are more recognizable today than the institutions in whose company they developed, and thus are given more attention. They are not, however, assessed for their abstract validity, but are presented for their importance as a central component of Chinese civilization.

This book is intended for use within the university or college as background reading to accompany a world history course, or general courses on traditional China, or as introductory reading in support of courses that may present in more detail later periods of Chinese history. If it serves also to introduce the subject of China to other readers of history and to direct them to more scholarly and more original further readings, it will have fulfilled its author's hopes.

A student of Chinese history offering a synthetic review of highlights of that vast subject can scarcely list all the intellectual debts he has acquired. The failure to acknowledge all these debts more specifically is thus a matter of acknowledging the impossible and not one of intellectual arrogance. But certain assistance in the preparation of this book must be noted. Two Princeton colleagues of great erudition and equally great common sense about writing have read the entire manuscript and offered invaluable advice on both form and content. They are Jeanette Mirsky, Fellow of the East Asian Studies Department, and Frank A. Kierman, Jr., Director of Research in the Chinese Linguistics Project. Another colleague, Professor Wei-ming Tu, offered perceptive advice on many technical points in Chinese intellectual history, in which he is deeply learned. To these colleagues, my warm thanks for generous help.

Most of the work of writing was accomplished during a semester when I was a Fellow of the Council for the Humanities at Princeton, and thanks are due the Council for generous support that freed me from most of my teaching duties during that semester.

Finally, to James S. K. Tung, Special Assistant University Librarian for Asian Collections at Princeton, thanks are due for all those indispensable services that in a great and smoothly functioning library we tend to take too much for granted; without those services our efforts to study and to teach could not even exist.

Prefatory Note for Revised Edition   During the seventeen years this book has been in print, colleagues using it in teaching, students in their courses, and reader friends of other sorts have brought to my attention ways in which it could be improved. In this revision I have gratefully responded to many of their suggestions. Also, archeological discoveries and scholarship in related fields have provided new information, stimulating much thought and reevaluation. If anything, the awareness that China's early history is directly relevant to our understanding of the present has grown, within China and abroad. I hope that this small book in this revised version will continue to be helpful to those seeking understanding of China and of ourselves.

Finally, I am grateful to my distinguished colleague, Ch'en Ta-tuan, for the calligraphy that graces the cover, title page, and chapter headings.

F. W. M.

Contents

Introduction

Most early writers of universal history adopted one of two tactics: They wrote the story of their own civilization and called it a history of the world, or they wrote theological history, the story of how God ruled his earthly kingdom. Medieval Western historians did both at once. They identified their own past with the history of the human race and gave it meaning and value by believing that this past was the expression of a providential plan.

Early efforts to write universal history failed because humans had no common past. The pre-Columbian civilizations of America attained their splendor in total isolation from the rest of the world. Although the many different ancient peoples living around the Mediterranean were often in close touch with one another, they had little knowledge about civilizations elsewhere. The Chinese knew accurately no other high civilization. Until the nineteenth century, they regarded the ideals of their own culture as normative for the entire world. Medieval Europe, despite fruitful contact with the Islamic world, was a closed society.

The fifteenth-century European voyages of discovery began a new era in the relations between Europe and the rest of the world. Between 1600 and 1900, Europeans displaced the populations of three other continents, conquered India, partitioned Africa, and decisively influenced the historical development of China and Japan. The expansion of Europe over the world gave Western historians a unifying theme: the story of how the non-Western world became the economic hinterland, political satellite, and technological debtor of Europe. Despite an enormously increased knowledge of the religions, arts and literatures, social structures, and political institutions of non-Western peoples, Western historians wrote a universal history that remained radically provincial. Only their assumptions changed. Before 1500 these assumptions were theological; by the nineteenth century they were indistinguishable from those of intelligent colonial governors.

The decline of European dominance, the rise to power of hitherto peripheral Western countries, such as the United States and the Soviet Union, and of non-Western ones, such as China and Japan, and the emergence of a world economy and a state-system embracing the planet have all created further options and opened wider perspectives. Historians of the future will be able to write real world history because for good and ill the world has begun to live a single history. And while this makes it no easier than before to understand and write the history of the world's remoter past, contemporary realities and urgencies have widened our curiosity and enlarged our sympathies, made less provincial our notion of what is relevant in the world's past, and taught us to study non-Western civilizations with fewer ethnocentric preconceptions. One of the intellectual virtues of our time is the effort to combine a conviction of the relativism of our own past and present beliefs with an affirmation of the civilizing value of the study of non-Western cultures. Among teaching historians good evidence of this commitment has been the wish to include non-Western materials in the traditional Western Civilization survey course and the growing interest in teaching World Civilization.

Professor Mote's book on the intellectual foundations of Chinese civilization is one in a series of twelve paperbacks to be published under the title *Studies in World Civilization*. One study will be devoted to modern China. Of the ten other studies in the series, one book will deal with early and one book with modern developments in Japan, India, Africa, Latin America, and the Middle East. The purpose of the series is to help teachers to use non-Western materials more effectively and to introduce college students as early as possible in their careers to the historical experience of peoples not commonly studied in survey courses on Western civilization.

History is long: The academic year lasts about thirty weeks. This disparity is one reason why survey courses tend to devote most of their time to studying the past of our own Western Civilization. The same disparity suggests the desirability of approaching non-Western history on a comparative basis. Professor Mote's brilliant essay illustrates the double advantage of this procedure. On the one hand, it describes an intellectual tradition different from our own and suggests that in order to understand it we must scan its history with humility and sophistication, abandoning implicit analogies with our own civilization and laying aside some of our most fundamental assumptions about time, space, causality, human nature, and history. On the other hand, it requires us—and helps us—to make explicit and self-conscious those very assumptions of our own intellectual tradition we now recognize to be radically different from the Chinese. To learn, for example, that the Chinese have had no real creation myth is to perceive more clearly the extent to which the Old Testament conception of a creative God has shaped Western thought. To grasp some of the preconceptions of Chinese cosmogony is to become more alert to the preconceptions of Western science. In short, familiarity with Chinese patterns of thought is a good in itself, pleasurable and instructive, like all good history; while, at the same time, knowledge of this alien and humane tradition usefully sharpens our understanding of ourselves.

EUGENE RICE
Columbia University

Chapter One
The Historical Beginnings

The foundations of a civilization are of several kinds: material, spiritual, social, and institutional. The material ones include man himself and the setting in which he lives; the others represent man's cumulative achievement in that setting, his response to its demands and to his own. Important as environmental factors have been, the unique patterns of Chinese life cannot adequately be explained by the struggle to maintain order while wresting a livelihood from the soil, for that was the common problem of early man everywhere. The geographer George B. Cressey has observed some ways in which the Chinese patterns have been distinctive.

More people have lived in China than anywhere else. Upwards of 10 billion human beings have moved across her good earth; nowhere else have so many people lived so intimately with nature. A thousand generations have left their indelible impress on soil and topography, so that scarcely a square foot of earth remains unmodified by man. With so many people to be fed, only the most painstaking care can provide an adequate harvest. Few landscapes are more human. It is also obvious that climate and topography have influenced the pattern of life. . . . Other lands are older, but none have

developed a more mature adjustment between man and the
environment.*

Writers have applied all kinds of environmental determinism to
Chinese history. One historian of Chinese thought, Fung Yu-lan, has
said that the landlocked character of China's agrarian life determined
the fundamental concepts of the early thinkers: The soil-bound agricultural life was concerned with real values rather than with abstract
concepts; the environmental conditions were not conducive to commerce, which in other early civilizations induced concern for numbers
and abstract mathematical concepts; the forms of agricultural production produced family-centered values and promoted cooperative rather
than individualistic and competitive norms; the consciousness of the
natural cycle enhanced the role of nature in the value scheme, and so
forth. This is a very interesting view. Yet such simplistically determinis-
tic views have their faults as total explanations. This one fails, among
other things, to point out how consequence can become cause in a
spiraling development that makes cause and effect difficult to distinguish.

Agriculture became a supreme value in the Chinese scheme, and
that was indeed an effect of the environment. But it also became a
supreme cause, a motive force in the further development of Chinese
civilization. As an established value, it competed against other values.
The high place of the farmer in Chinese idealizations of society reflects
this. The moral value set upon agriculture as the proper activity of an
honest man also reflects it, and that value helped prevent the use of
human effort, water and water power, and animals on "nonproduc-
tive" and dubious undertakings like commerce and industry. So what
determined what? But our concern here is not to argue a theory of
history; rather it is to call attention to the setting and to stress the
distinctive character of the Chinese accommodation to it.

Any consideration of the ecological circumstances of early human
life in East Asia shows the material factors to be inextricably bound
up with other elements of the civilization Chinese men and women
produced there. In addition to those material foundations, there are

* George B. Cressey. *The Land of the Five Hundred Million: A Geography of China*. New
York: McGraw-Hill, 1955, p. 3.

also the spiritual foundations, that is, the nonmaterial components of Chinese life to consider. These took form, on the one hand, as the concepts, the attitudes, the values, and the cumulative knowledge which the Chinese people, having generated some and borrowed others, put to use in that setting. On the other hand, the nonmaterial foundations of the civilization also include the social and institutional forms, products of the long interaction of human and material resources and of guiding ideas.

The history of how all these constituent elements of Chinese civilization developed is a very long one, extending back into a time for which we have only shreds of documentation, that is, into East Asian prehistory. It may even extend back to stages of human or protohuman development in East Asia that we have no particular reason to call Chinese. The riddle here involves not merely that usual question about when the accepted name for a high civilization should begin to apply to its early antecedents. One of the most intriguing riddles of all human history is where the earliest stage of China's high civilization came from—the stage at which Chinese writing and Chinese bronze technology first appeared either as inventions or as borrowings. Many authorities stress the continuity of Chinese civilization and its relative isolation from other equally advanced civilizations as the elements that account most significantly for China's special character. What does historical "Chineseness" then consist of? Can we identify the point in history at which "China" begins?

The high Chinese civilization is characterized for us perhaps most pertinently by its possession of the Chinese written language. That first literate stage of Chinese civilization emerged into verifiable history between 2000 and 1500 B.C.—a period from which we have archeologically recovered material remains, including literary material, in great profusion. Yet that civilization's immediate antecedents are simply unclear. Archeologists working throughout the last forty years have found many material remains of early Chinese divination practices that utilized the shoulder blades of animals and the shells of tortoises. These relatively durable "oracle-bone" materials, inscribed with divination texts, were found by the thousands in the 1920s and 1930s in sites excavated in Honan Province in the North China Plain. They have been firmly identified with the Shang-Yin period (ca. 1500–1100 B.C.) by the content of the oracles, naming a full sequence of Shang kings who occupied their last capital at the city called Yin. The oracle-bone script is a well-developed writing system, one assumed to have gone through a thousand or more years of development. It was found in conjunction with a bronze technology that astounds us, both in point of the casting techniques and the artistic conception. The late Shang people were the heirs of an old civilization. The assumption about the long history of their script has in fact been confirmed. The Academy of Social Sciences in Peking announced in 1986 an exciting discovery from a site near modern Sian in Northwest China: oracle bones bearing script and archeologically dated to the period 3000 to 2500 B.C., thus antedating not just the late Yin phase of Shang but the entire Shang period. Moreover the newly found script is described as clearly an earlier, more primitive stage in the development of the oracle-bone script of Shang.

This latest material evidence for the earlier stages of the script, coupled with other recent archeological finds from throughout the entire region of modern China, more or less lay to rest older views that this particular invention of writing, apparently one of the two or three independent inventions of full scripts in human history, and the related bronze technology, might not be Chinese but were diffused from other parts of the world. We no longer have strong reasons for questioning an independent East Asian invention of these things. Certainly we should not overlook the fact of the distinctiveness of the entire cultural complex of which they are part. Although the stages furnishing the evidence for the earliest development of the script, for example, are not directly known to us yet, there are many cultural links between that civilization in which we first find writing and the still earlier, nonliterate, neolithic cultures of the same region, cultures also well known to archeology. Some of the foundations of traditional China had already begun to take shape in those early prehistoric phases too.

But history proper, in China as elsewhere, is considered to begin with written materials. Oracle-bone texts yield ever-richer understanding of ancient China as experts now decipher and interpret them. Their information often can be linked to the fuller historical documentation from the first millennium B.C. Old Chinese historical accounts in documents dating from about 1000 B.C.—to the considerable surprise of skeptical historians—have been remarkably well confirmed by the past half-century of archeological research. This now leads many historians to anticipate that the whole tradition concerning still earlier epochs, particularly those detailing the succession of kings of the Hsia dynasty (for which the legendary dates are ca. 2200–1700 B.C.) and the pre-Yin phases of the Shang dynasty (roughly 1760–1500 B.C.) may well also someday be verified by archeology. In fact some of the extensive archeology conducted in mainland China in the past forty years bears importantly on Shang culture, but oracle bones with inscriptions or other forms of writing making the identification explicit seem not to have turned up yet. Until that happens or until other kinds of material evidence become more complete, the precise story of Chinese origins must remain a fascinating but tantalizing puzzle, providing cultural historians with enticing opportunities to indulge in speculation and hypothesis.

Let us, however, accept the last Shang civilization dating from about 1500 B.C. as a starting point. Since it is well anchored in material evidence supplemented by much further historical and legendary written material, we can speak with considerable certainty about that earliest substantiated phase of Chinese history. These earliest foundations of the civilization are already "Chinese" in significant ways. The Shang state was at that time already aware of itself as a "central kingdom" of high culture, a nuclear area conscious of peripheral peoples showing lesser cultural attainment, but peoples susceptible to Shang's civilizing influences. It occupied a small area (only the size of modern France) in the central and lower Yellow River drainage traditionally regarded as the heartland of ancient China. Shang economy was based on intensive village agriculture of a kind made possible by the environmental circumstances of North China, circumstances especially of water and soil and climate and terrain that have remained largely the same throughout history.

Shang civilization displayed specialization in the manufacture of its craft products. It had achieved what archeologists call mature urbanism. It engaged in a wide trade facilitated by the use of cowrie-shell currency. Its bronze technology has scarcely been equaled in subsequent ages in any part of the world. Its use of silk, jade, and other luxury materials showed considerable sophistication. An elaborate ceremonial based on lineage and on concepts of ancestor worship marked its stratified social organization and its complex political life. The archeologist Kwang-chih Chang concludes that the Yin-Shang civilization was indeed a new phenomenon, the outcome of vast and thorough change, so that with it the Neolithic Age ended, and Chinese history truly begins.

Moreover he asserts that the Shang civilization developed from elements already present on Chinese soil. It is now demonstrated that bronze technology, writing, and chariot warfare, the three elements which, because of analogies to Western Asian cultural features, are most susceptible to the interpretation that they were not indigenous to China, could have been of East Asian origin. Most scholars now assume them to have been purely indigenous developments, even though very recently there has emerged archeological evidence pointing to several locations in East and Southeast Asia as possible sites of the important late-Neolithic advances in civilization. But also the historian P. T. Ho has published (in Chinese) a monumental study of the origins of Chinese agriculture, demonstrating through its highly distinctive features how unlikely it is that early Chinese civilization could have represented a diffusion of culture from India, the Fertile Crescent, or other early centers of civilization.

Regardless of how that archeological puzzle is eventually solved, the further advances achieved by the Shang led directly to the maturation of Chinese civilization in the nine hundred year long Chou dynasty that followed. Some scholars would go further and state that Shang art, for example, gave rise to and inspired the major art tradition of the whole Pacific basin. And it increasingly becomes clear that the nuclear area of Shang was the central point from which bronze metallurgy, agricultural advances, and perhaps a complex of spiritual and social elements were diffused not just throughout the Chinese culture area but also to all of East and Southeast Asia.

Historical analogies always have serious shortcomings; nonetheless a suggestive if ultimately inaccurate one is that the Chou people were the Romans of the ancient Chinese cultural world. They were a peripheral people with martial qualities and a genius for government who burst in upon a nuclear area in some respects Greek-like, appropriated its esthetic and philosophical achievements, and amalgamated it into their own state and society, thus producing a new stage in the growth of the civilization. Some scholars have even gone so far as to suggest that the Chou conquest, not merely of Shang, but of the whole central area corresponding to all modern China north of the Yangtze, forced an amalgamation of cultural strands that produced a fundamentally new civilization. Were we to accept this view of the Chou conquest, we could not then really speak of "Chinese civilization" until after the new cultural mix had resulted from the imposition of Chou hegemony. If, as seems probable, this view ultimately is rejected because it underes-

timates the continuity of cultural forms from Shang to Chou, it
nonetheless correctly calls attention to the importance of the Chou
conquest. It extended the influence of the central cultural area and
incorporated an enlarged and growing territory into the nuclear zone
of early Chinese culture.

The analogy of Greece and Rome to Shang and Chou is misleading
in one essential respect. Chou China was linguistically close to Shang
and had adopted the same written form of their common language
even before the conquest in 1111 B.C. (if indeed we ultimately settle
on that date for that event—the chronology is slightly uncertain prior
to the eighth century B.C.). And Chou, border feudatory of Shang
before the conquest, unlike Rome vis-à-vis Greece, had been culturally
and politically Shang's subsidiary. When Chou conquered the center
of the world (for such it was in the view of all concerned), it succeeded
eagerly to all the pretensions that went with control of the center of
the world's single culture area. Chou aspired to moral and political
legitimacy in that successor role rather than to the role of an alien
conqueror. It had no self-doubt in assuming it, and in its cultural
propaganda stressed the common antecedents of the two states as heirs
to a highly mythologized antiquity that had spawned both their dynastic lines. More successfully than the Shang predecessors had, the Chou
court imposed on all the rest of the burgeoning Chinese world its court
language and ceremonial, the distinctively Chou political devices, and
the common cultural standards of Shang and Chou, as well as the
ideological bases of Chou claims to political legitimacy. It accomplished this by creating a pattern of political relationships deceptively
similar to European feudalism. The Chou founder and his immediate
successor (Kings Wen and Wu) gave about fifty important fiefs to their
clan members and relatives by marriage, strategically placing them to
garrison important locations. They further dispensed about twenty
more to their chief associates in the conquest. The Shang heirs were
granted an important fief, Sung, to permit them to perpetuate their
ancestral rites, for they too had once been legitimate rulers of China.
Beyond these seventy-odd feudal states there may have been as many
as two hundred other local lords who were confirmed in the control
of their tiny territories. The majority of these were so small and unimportant that their names scarcely appear in the historical materials.
The number of these steadily diminished. By the eighth century B.C.
the total of all states may have been about 150, of which 25 mattered.

And by the fourth century the annexation process had gone so far that there remained only Royal Chou, which by then hardly mattered in power terms, seven large, important, and now virtually autonomous feudatories, and no more than a handful of the remnants of the other states.

The central domain of the Chou kings wielded an overawing military supremacy for no more than the first quarter of the Chou dynastic history. It was militarily insignificant after 770 B.C., the year border wars and barbarian incursions from Inner Asia forced the transfer of its capital from the Wei River site (modern Sian) to the east (modern Loyang). Yet the Chou court continued to exercise a nominal hegemony for five hundred years more; its power derived from a mystique of legitimacy that the founding Chou figures had carefully established and that Chou civilization nurtured and enhanced.

It was not until 256 B.C. that another state dared openly to depose the reigning Chou king, and then to use its vast and effectively mobilized military strength to impose unification on all of China progressively through the decade from 230 to 220 B.C. This was the state of Ch'in. As successor to the Chou and ruler of a newly united China, it gave its name to the brief dynastic period (221–204 B.C.) that begins the imperial era of Chinese history.

But before the Chinese empire took form, the late centuries of the Chou period produced a Golden Age of Chinese thought. The base layer of the ideological foundations of Chinese history is largely a product of the three or four centuries beginning about the time of Confucius (born 551 B.C.) and ending with the Ch'in conquest in 221 B.C. The ideas that occupied the Chinese mind of that age, together with some of the related social and political elements of the Chou civilization, merit our thoughtful consideration, for to a very large degree they have molded all subsequent Chinese history.

Chapter Two

The Beginnings of a World View

The Chinese did not possess writing as early as the ancient Near East. Even though we have new material evidence for the existence of Chinese writing in the third millennium B.C., Sumer in the Near East possessed writing one thousand or more years before China. The second-millennium Cretans (equivalent to Shang dynasty) were beginning to develop linear alphabetic scripts from hieroglyphics; they left these for the early Greeks to complete, and via the Phoenicians this invention became the common property of the whole Mediterranean world. And yet even by the Homeric age (ninth century B.C.) the Greeks had produced very little in the way of written records that was to remain central to their civilization. Assur is famous for the great libraries of the seventh century B.C., and still earlier Egypt and Babylon had acquired the habit of storing up records. Yet these civilizations died, and the body of materials they recorded had no active role in later civilizations. The Aryan invaders of India, contemporaries of the late Shang and the early Chou dynasties in China, brought the Vedas to the Indian subcontinent. These classical religious works gave form to Indian civilization. But the Aryans were illiterate, and India did not begin to accumulate a significant body of writings, including the writing down of the Vedas, until the sixth century B.C., and nothing has survived that dates from earlier than the third century B.C., by which time vast quantities of writings, many extant today, were essential to the daily life of the Chinese civilization.

It is therefore probably correct to say that none of the earlier civilizations has left a body of literary materials from the first half of the first millennium so broad in its range as those coming to us from preimperial China, and perhaps none is so great in quantity either. Certainly no early civilization gave greater attention to writing and to study of its written records. If ancient China was not literate as early as some other parts of the world, it was "literary" in degree and quality far beyond other early civilizations.

To be sure, Confucius (born 551 B.C.) left his own thoughts to be written down by his followers as the *Analects* of the master, but that is because, intent on the study of the literary heritage venerated by his age, his own thoughts presumably seemed to him not worthy of preserving in writing. He traveled from one feudal capital to another to examine archives of texts that might supplement those of his own native state and provide him with better versions of annals and rituals and those other extensive bodies of texts which had become revered and much studied by his time. Much of this material did not survive the destructive wars and political policies of the third century B.C. Yet in addition to the simple and brief oracle-bone texts and later inscriptions found on bronze vessels, we possess a number of "books" that were written in the early Chou period, either in their entirety or as major portions of canons that assumed their present form in later centuries. These include the *Book of Changes* (*I Ching*), the *Odes* or *Classic of Poetry* (the *Shih Ching*, in Arthur Waley's translation called *The Book of Songs*), and the *Documents* or *Classic of History* (*Shang Shu*, *Shu Ching*, or *Shu*), as well as extensive annals and books recording and explaining ritual practices. The focus upon these as objects of study, as repositories of accumulated human wisdom, and as the traditions of learned commentary and explication shows to what an extent China was a civilization of writing and of written monuments at a very early time. Of all the foregoing works, the *Book of Changes* has exerted the most continually pervasive, stimulating influence on Chinese thought. Today it has become an element of world civilization, if a somewhat misused one.

Book of Changes

Any brief comment on the Book of Changes is inadequate to suggest the levels of significance that can be assigned to it. It is a book of divination texts, apparently embodying the Chou traditions in divination methods and concepts (as distinct from the earlier Shang tradition utilizing oracle bones). At the same time, it heralds a striking cosmology and a philosophy of human potential for creative action and freedom in the cosmic process. Some modern thinkers have found it possesses considerable value; the psychologist Carl Jung, for example, found the work to be of uncommon significance as a method of exploring the unconscious. If, as is probable, the bare divination texts (without the lengthy explanations) go back to twelfth-century Chou oral traditions, they assumed their present written form perhaps as late as the seventh century B.C. Those texts and the further parts of the book have been continually augmented from the time of Confucius. The book has grown and matured as a philosophy along with Chinese civilization and has remained a bottomless well from which each age of Chinese thought has drawn provocative insight. As the horizons of Chinese philosophy have broadened, so has the meaning of this book assumed a subtlety adequate to whatever demands the Chinese mind has made upon it. Yet it is not just a "wisdom book" like those in some other cultures, a book whose ultimate value is only that of effectively distilled common sense. In attempting to say much more, the Book of Changes teeters on the brink between profound awareness of the human mind's capacities and superficial incoherency; nothing about it is simple and straightforward. The incongruencies are themselves essential to its purposes. A typical example is the following:

The Text of Number 32: Heng/Duration
THE JUDGMENT
Duration. Success. No blame.
Perseverance furthers.
It furthers one to have somewhere to go.
THE IMAGE
Thunder and wind: the image of Duration.

Thus the superior man stands firm
And does not change his direction.*

This, of course, is but a portion of the content relevant to this particular divination text; it is cited merely to show the nature of the language. Can one make intelligent use of ideas stated in this fashion? Should we brush it all aside as simple-minded nonsense? There have always been individuals in the history of Chinese thought who have been willing to do so, but they are not consistently the clearest-minded or the most profound of Chinese thinkers. On the contrary, the concern with the uses and meaning of this book has been a feature of the thought of a majority of China's great philosophers, and its central place has been reaffirmed in each age.

We must therefore take the *Book of Changes* quite seriously as one of the earliest crystallizations of the Chinese mind (or of the human mind in its universal characteristics). We should try to understand what about it has so unfailingly fascinated thinking Chinese from ancient times onward, and on that score regard it as one touchstone of what is peculiarly Chinese. As a historical document its greatest significance to us is perhaps that it conveys the earliest awareness of a world view that was later to become much more complete and explicit. This Chinese conception of the world has scarcely ever been recognized by Westerners and still is not properly noted, much less borne in mind, in most of the writings on China.

The Chinese World View

The manner in which cultures become aware of other cultures and the extent to which persons in one culture insert elements of their own culture into their understanding of others can nowhere be better illustrated than by noting the Western failure to understand the basic nature of the Chinese world view. Modern Europeans and Americans have insisted on making the unexamined and, as it turns out, quite

---

* I Ching, or Book of Changes. Translated into English by Cary F. Baynes from the German translation of Richard Wilhelm. Foreword by Carl Jung and Prefaces by Richard and Hellmut Wilhelm. Bollingen Series, vol. 19 (Princeton, N.J.: Princeton University Press, 1967), pp. 126–127.

unsupportable assumption that all peoples (until modern science and Western thinking in the last century affected cosmological theorizing—that is, theorizing about what the cosmos is—throughout the world) have regarded the cosmos and the human race as the products of a creator external to them. Assuming fundamental analogy as a fact, Westerners in translating Chinese texts have simply relied on falsely analogous expressions from our culture and have read them mechanically into the Chinese texts, perhaps satisfying themselves with the "sense" that they make in the way they echo our Western predilections.

Confucius' apparent intimations of Christian truth in the eyes of seventeenth-century and later missionaries are therefore as myopic, as assessments of intellectual and cultural developments in history, as are Aristotle's in the eyes of Aquinas. But when twentieth-century historians perpetuate such myopia, it is no longer tolerable. Rather it should be very interesting to us to discover what new and deeper understanding of China we may be led to by an objective understanding of Chinese cosmological thinking, once our sense of Chinese culture has been freed from the imposition of our own.

The basic point which outsiders have found so hard to detect is that the Chinese, among all peoples ancient and recent, primitive and modern, are apparently unique in having no creation myth, that is, they have regarded the world and humans as uncreated, as constituting the central features of a spontaneously self-generating cosmos having no creator, god, ultimate cause, or will external to itself. If this belief was ever otherwise, even in the earliest periods of Chinese history, no evidence for it has persisted to influence later Chinese thinking. Moreover other fundamentally different cosmogonies (explanations of the genesis of the cosmos) presenting the idea of creation and a creator external to the created world made no significant impression on the Chinese mind when encountered among South China minorities or in successive contact with Indian, Islamic, and Christian thought. Their own conception of the world, shared subsequently by all Chinese schools of thought on the level of the Great Tradition*—and it is a conception having pervasive influence throughout the entire soci-

---

* Great Tradition, a term here used loosely to designate the high culture of learning and elite tradition.

ety—has been developed throughout the continuous cultural history of the Chinese people without any fundamental modification other than its refinement and more detailed articulation.

The Confucian scholar Tu Wei-ming, in an essay reviewing and emending the ideas just set forth, argues that the distinctiveness of the Chinese world view comes less from the lack of any notion of creation external to the cosmos (for he believes there may be other examples, perhaps among preliterate peoples) than from the other half of the concept, the organismic wholeness and interconnectedness of all being. He writes: ". . . the apparent lack of a creation myth in Chinese cultural history is predicated on a more fundamental assumption about reality; namely, that all modalities of being are organically connected." In his view the "spontaneously self-generating life process exhibits three basic motifs: continuity, wholeness, and dynamism." His elaboration of these ideas is essentially Neo-Confucian in content and draws on a number of Neo-Confucian thinkers, showing the continued importance of organismic cosmological conceptions into later history. He fully agrees however that from our point of view, as Westerners who have inherited the Judeo-Christian ideas about the creation of the world by a creator God, we have difficulties in setting aside the assumptions that go with that kind of cosmogony and comprehending the implications of the quite radically different Chinese views.*

The historical evidence concerning creation myths in early China (down to the third century B.C.) has been summed up and evaluated by Derk Bodde. He notes that in the whole range of early Chinese myths and of myths present in early China, only the P'an-ku legend can be called a creation story. But this was an obscure tale in early China, if indeed it was known at all. Why has this story become important in our time? A probable answer is that Chinese in the past century or more have been repeatedly asked, "What is China's creation story?" by outsiders who have assumed that all civilizations must explain the existence of the world in conceptually analogous ways. Realizing what the outsiders want, the Chinese have found the P'an-ku

---

* Tu Wei-ming. "The Continuity of Being: Chinese Visions of Nature." Reprinted in Tu Wei-ming, *Confucian Thought: Selfhood as Creative Transformation*. Albany, N.Y.: State University Press of New York, 1985, pp. 35–53. The quotations are found on pages 35 and 38.

story the most convenient reply. But we must remember that the question itself was not a set question in the traditional civilization, and the Chinese traditionally did not formulate their central ideas in response to alien questions. Bodde has demonstrated that the P'an-ku legend was late in making its appearance in China, not being known in any records that can be dated before the third century A.D. By that time China's distinctive cosmogony had long been fully worked out. He shows, moreover, that the alien origin of the legend must be assumed. It probably came from India where a very similar creation story is known, though there are also parallels that could have been the source of the Chinese version in the legends of the Miao (Meo) people of South China and Southeast Asia.

As stated earlier "cosmology" is the effort to conceptualize what the world, or the cosmos, is and "cosmogony" is an explanation of how the cosmos came into being. Cosmologies and cosmogonies range from primitive myths to modern physics. Ancient China's cosmology and cosmogony seem somehow closer to the explanations offered by modern physics than to those we find in myths and religious systems. Yet that is not to suggest that the ancient Chinese were "scientific" beyond their time; it would be more accurate to suggest that their curious and unique conceptualizations happen to be suggestive of modern scientific explanations, but that they were arrived at by quite different intellectual routes.

The genuine Chinese cosmogony is that of organismic process, meaning that all the parts of the entire cosmos belong to one organic whole and that they all interact as participants in one spontaneously self-generating life process. Recently Joseph Needham and Wang Ling have provided the contemporary terminology and concepts with which to explain the Chinese cosmology to modern Western minds. Yet the field of China studies has been slow to respond to this aspect of their work. The older, misleading analogies to Western conceptions continue to appear in writings and in translations of old Chinese texts. Yet even before Needham and Wang extensively demonstrated the nature and the implications of Chinese cosmological thinking, the distinctiveness of the Chinese world conception had been noticed by some authorities. In 1949 Jung had noted: "The ancient Chinese mind contemplates the cosmos in a way comparable to that of the modern physicist, who cannot deny that his model of the world is a decidedly psychophysical structure."* Needham, analyzing that Chinese model, calls it "an ordered harmony of wills without an ordainer."† As he describes the *organismic* Chinese cosmos, it emerges to our full view as one in striking contrast to all other world conceptions known to human history. It differs from other organismic conceptions, such as classic Greek cosmologies in which a *logos* or demiurge or otherwise conceived master will external to creation was regarded as necessary for existence. And it contrasts still more strikingly with the ancient Semitic traditions that led to subsequent Christian and Islamic conceptions of creation *ex nihilo* by the hand of God, or through the will of God, and all other such mechanistic, teleological, and theistic cosmologies. Our civilization has been so long content in those narrow confines that we have found it next to impossible even to comprehend the wholly different nature of the traditional Chinese world view.

Bodde and Needham have fully demonstrated that a distinctive Chinese cosmology exists, and indeed many scholars of the past century have indicated their awareness of the essential aspects of the full story. The evidence is overwhelming, but it has not been so much challenged as simply ignored. If we are to take it seriously, we must ask the questions about what relevance a culture's cosmological orientations should be expected to have for the other aspects of its history.

Implications of Chinese Cosmogony

If we believe, as the Chinese have believed, that people more or less consciously make their own history, we might expect this distinctive aspect of Chinese consciousness to bear some relationship to the areas of Chinese history that are different from our own. Or noting this essential point of distinctiveness in the ideological realm, we may then be able to discover related differences that we have failed to note heretofore. The implications of China's world view for all aspects of Chinese history merit some exploratory thinking and speculation. The

---

* I Ching, p. xxiv.

† Joseph Needham and Wang Ling. *Science and Civilization in China*, vol. 2, p. 287. 16 vols. to date. Cambridge: Cambridge University Press, 1954–.

following seven points of possible relevance may serve to indicate the scope and significance of the issue.

CHINESE SPIRITS AND "GODS"   The early Chinese, and in fact Chinese of all ages, have accepted the view that "spiritual" beings exist. They are spiritual in the sense that they somehow exist apart from normal human life, but material in that they represent different states of matter. Spirits of deceased persons continue to linger about, the lighter and heavier parts of their noncorporeal selves having separated from the corpse at the moment breath (ch'i, or "spirit") left it. These then separately go their more terrestrial or more ethereal ways for a time (on the basis of affinity between their substance and earth or air), until they at last return indistinguishably again into the flux of universal matter. By that time, if not sooner, they have lost all traces of the individual's identity. This is an essentially naturalistic conception, in that it describes "spirit" as having the same qualities and as being subject to the same processes as all other aspects of nature. It is true that in the vulgarized versions of this rather philosophical conception, spirits sometimes began to resemble "gods." They were also somewhat colored in later ages by vulgarized Buddhist notions of transmigration and karma. Even those alien notions adapted more to Chinese views than the other way around.

The speculative issue is that whatever spiritual beings or spiritual forces the ancient Chinese were apt to acknowledge and venerate, by the limitations of their cosmology, none was capable of being dignified above all others as something external to the cosmos and therefore not subject to its dynamic process or as the ultimate cause behind it all, responsible for existence. If no supergod could be granted such a function, then the prime impulse toward monotheism was lacking. But monotheism becomes necessary only where a particular concept of casuality is accepted. Modern writers such as Carl Jung and Hellmut Wilhelm have noted in their discussion of the Book of Changes the West's preference for "causality" and China's for "synchronicity," which are fundamentally different explanations of the relationships among events.

Western scholars tend to assume that all religions show parallel tendencies and that higher religions are those that have succeeded in becoming monotheistic. The Chinese example seems to make such assumptions irrelevant because Chinese religion simply was not on that track. China produced little that resembles what in other high cultures scholars have usually called the mature development of religion and no tendencies toward monotheism at all. Moreover the lesser gods and spirits that the Chinese did venerate, on various levels of their culture and for various reasons, tended to merge with other aspects of nature and retain less separate significance than their counterparts elsewhere (for example, animistic cult objects, saints, members of the innumerable pantheons of other cultures). This suggests that highly generalized statements about culture derived from observations of other cultures should not be unquestioningly applied and that what has been described as primitive polytheism or rudimentary pantheism in Chinese popular religion may signify something else. By mid-Chou times there had occurred a development clearly reflected in the early works such as the *Book of Changes:* The concept of *t'ien*, called heaven or nature, which had been an anthropomorphic conception of a deified ancestor a millennium earlier, had become an abstract conception of cosmic function. This change reflects what many scholarly works have described as an apparent but unexplained rise of rationalism in Chinese culture in this period. The Chinese world view, properly understood, offers much help in explaining this. Other features of Chinese religion also can be better understood when freed from implicit assumptions about universal analogies in the way people think.

All the foregoing discussion of gods and spirits or of Chinese conceptions that might be translated by those loosely used English terms, may depict the Chinese as "more rational" than other peoples. To some extent that may be the consequence of our modern preference for rationality imposing itself on the phenomena we study; in short, as moderns we see rationality because we hope to find it. Insofar as we make that error our argument for greater rationality in Chinese conceptions of spiritual forces and beings would be defective. In general however it is hard to escape the feeling that early Chinese thought was less concerned with fervid religiosity and with the nonrational modes of dealing with life's uncertainties than were many other early civilizations. That is, regardless of how members of the upper echelons of Chinese society, the group we know most about, may themselves have felt about such things as death and immortality, or benevolent and malevolent spirits, the Chinese high tradition did not encourage them to invoke otherworldly powers, for there were none. All phenomena were of this world, and there was reasonable hope of explaining or understanding them even if, as in Taoism, the understanding might defy verbalization. Much less did that high tradition, as we encounter it in the formal philosophizing, declare that the reasoning mind should grant higher value to truths that must be accepted on faith alone, as did Christianity and other religions. St. Thomas Aquinas developed Aristotelian rationality to the utmost in formulating his five ways of knowing that God exists, but still held that the believer must go beyond those ways to accept God's existence on faith. To him this ultimate tenet of the religious life is a matter of belief, not reason. The Chinese Great Tradition, under no necessity to consider the issue of a supreme creator God, did not need to elevate faith over reason. Stressing rational arguments in, above all, ethical and social issues, its intellectual problems were seldom extended into realms that demanded faith in truths that could not be reached by the various ways of knowing.

That is not to say that the Chinese were not aware of and often highly favorable toward intuitive knowledge. Intuition is not reason, for the process by which one intuitively knows is not subject to analysis and reasoned understanding. Nonetheless to intuit is to know and to know with great certainty (even should the knowledge so acquired prove to be erroneous); it is not like faith which demands that one believe without knowing. St. Thomas Aquinas, all his rationality notwithstanding, had a mystical religious experience a few months before his death; after that he declared that the certainty of knowledge he achieved through that intuitive knowing experience rendered his lifelong work of writing and formulating argumentation quite meaningless by comparison. He was not describing the leap of faith (which he held to be necessary for a believing Christian), but an experience of direct, immediate knowing. We shall see that some Chinese thinkers also accepted the validity of intuitive knowledge, some holding it to be equal to or superior to inference and reason and other rational modes of knowing via the senses and the reflecting mind. China's Great Tradition accepted different epistemologies, but it did not lend support to the manifold and widespread modes of believing and acting that by-passed the pursuit of knowledge, and most Chinese thinkers stressed the soberly rational ways of pursuing it. The truths of religion were no exception, at least at that high level of their pursuit.

IMPACT ON INSTITUTIONS   We can speak with much less certainty about the religious belief of the common people in early China than we can about the religious elements preserved in the documents of the Great Tradition. But it seems justified to say that any theistic tendencies in popular religious practices, or tendencies to elevate certain spirits to the level of general gods, must have been greatly weakened by the fact that the Great Tradition did not and, in its increasing rationalism through early Chou times, could not give any support to such tendencies. How remote from the lives of the ordinary people is a Great Tradition? Is it a crystallization of popular culture raised to a higher level of rationalization, or is it a counter force? For very early periods especially, it is difficult to know. Later on in imperial Chinese society, the belief in the active possibility of social mobility—perhaps even more than the actual statistical incidence of it—kept the different levels of cultural life highly coherent and congruent. Each level was an active model to be imitated by the one below. Hence China's Great Tradition, an antitheistic, nonteleological and essentially rational set of ideas, had a greater capacity to exert the influence of broadened versions of its essential characteristics upon popular culture than it would have had in a civilization with a closed society and a more rigidly stratified cultural form.

An open society, gradually achieved during the last preimperial centuries, coupled with the cosmological content of the Chinese Great Tradition, must also have worked to keep religion weak in all its formalized and institutionalized forms. That is not to imply that the early Chinese were irreligious, but that institutionalizing tendencies could not easily become important in the sphere of religion, and people's religion remained a matter of private and decentralized family practice, or at least of no more than local organization.

Institutionalizing tendencies, present in most religions as observed in most societies, were not very important among the Chinese for still another reason: Their cosmic process lacked a mechanistic concept. A cosmic dynamism like that conceived by the early Chinese, fully explicable in terms merely of its internal harmony and the balance among the parts of a conceptually known but also naturalistically observed world organism, does not lend itself to the development of formal social instrumentalities—of churches, or of political systems working alongside churches—for achieving goals that religion may define and sanction. Some religions provide the convenient analogy of a god who will assist the political order in restraining deviations from its norms. But in ancient China, the workings of harmony furnished no usefully explicit analogies for humans to imitate and provided no suprarational authority to be borrowed by those who might try to do so.

THE PROBLEM OF EVIL   The late Dr. Hu Shih, eminent historian of Chinese thought and culture, used to say with sly delight that centuries of Christian missionaries had been frustrated and chagrined by the apparent inability of Chinese to take sin seriously. Were we to work out fully all the consequences for Chinese society of the model offered by an organismic cosmos functioning through the dynamism of harmony, we might well be able to relate the absence of a sense of sin to it. For in such a cosmos there can be no parts wrongfully present; everything that exists belongs, even if no more appropriately than as the consequence of a temporary imbalance, a disharmony. Evil as a positive or active force cannot exist; much less can it be frighteningly personified. No devils can struggle with good forces for mastery of humans and the universe, and people's errors, unlike sin in other worlds, can neither offend personal gods nor threaten a person's individual existence. The question of immortality in a future that "really counts"—if one is lucky enough or good enough to transcend the material present reality—does not even arise. This being true in the Great Tradition, countertendencies in the popular religions in China's highly congruent culture were correspondingly weakened.

CONSEQUENCES OF A WORLD WITHOUT SIN   The consequence of such a definition of the problem of evil for the Chinese character seems to be something like the issue at stake in the frequently encountered distinction between shame cultures and guilt cultures. Whether this formula, derived by anthropologists from observations of relatively simple cultures, will have lasting value when applied to a civilization as complex as that of traditional China may be questioned. But it suggests that further hypotheses about Chinese national character and Chinese personality types might well be guided by some reference to a cosmology which apparently releases people from the mechanical workings of fear and sin doctrines, and offers them a less threatened and less threatening personal relationship to their cosmos. Yet Chinese ethical philosophy in all periods stresses the necessity to engage in self-examination and self-correction; the philosophic foundations for moral responsibility were not lacking.

THE SOURCES OF AUTHORITY   Let us extend this point to consider what it may have done to, or for, a whole people whose civilization lacks any sense of a creator-creature relationship. The individual in such a situation is not humbled before an omniscient, omnipresent, and omnipotent creator-ruler. In one sense, a Chinese man's or woman's relationship to his or her ancestors might seem to serve analogously. Yet the quality of such a relationship is radically different. For example, medieval Christians could escape a theoretically less-binding paternal authority by making a profession of serving the inescapable one of God the Father; sons who had or who wanted no place in a particular human family could join the clergy and be called Father by everyone. Chinese sons could not escape the responsibilities of filial submission in a sublimated or substitute way; even in the eyes of the state, filial responsibility had priority over loyalty to ruler and state. In which culture, it must be asked, was paternal authority the more binding? And which granted the individual the stronger sense of being his own master? It is easier to conclude that Chinese society should have reflected fundamental points of difference due to its different definitions of individual responsibility and of authority than it is to define these.

How, for example, did the Chinese cosmology provide any basis for the authority to make social and ethical norms effective? The relationship of Chinese cosmology to the theory and practice of law has been rather extensively debated and speculated upon. Yet perhaps more could be said about the lack of divinely revealed commandment in the Chinese cultural tradition and the effect of that lack upon the nature of law, since the contrast with our own cultural tradition at this point is so striking. In a civilization like the Chinese where there are only human sources (or, among the Taoists, "natural" sources) of authority, law could scarcely be expected to achieve the significance it possessed in civilizations where it was based on a superrational and unchallengeable law of God that commanded all creatures—and states as well—to enforce its literal prohibitions. Nor in China could there be any priestly enforcers of divine commandment, or even secular rulers enforcing divine law or civil law armed with the authority derived by some analogy between man's and God's laws. Clearly the widely different institutions of church and state derived some of their characteristics from the differing cosmological orientations of the societies in which they developed.

THE SECULAR HARMONIOUS WORLD   The all-enfolding harmony of impersonal cosmic function can be seen to serve analogous, yet qualitatively different, ends from those provided by cosmologies oriented toward a supreme power that knowingly directs the cosmos. The Chinese world view kept one's attention on life here and now and made Chinese thinkers responsible for ordaining the forms and patterns of that life. The ritualized society of China can be adequately explained only in terms of its own cosmology; the relationship of the one to the other is direct and primary. One might cite a wide spectrum of rather puzzling problems in Chinese cultural and social history, from the large and grave role assigned to the *Book of Changes* by so many of China's best and most social-minded thinkers, to the imperial government's seemingly inconsistent role, in view of the rational tone of its Great Tradition, in fostering a range of popular religious practices. These may seem less puzzling if we remember that the rituals of state, the auguries of the *Book of Changes*, and the popular religions tolerated by or even patronized by the state and the leaders of local society, all were *secular*. The forces they addressed (sincerely or otherwise) were forces of this world on a par with mankind as parts of the world of nature. The Chinese landscape has always been filled with venerated or fearsome spirits, demons, local gods, cult figures, and hungry ghosts. The state sought to formalize the people's relations to those, as it also was held to be responsible for supervising many of mankind's relations with the forces of nature in the organismic cosmos. Did it place strains on the philosophically grounded upholders of the high tradition to acknowledge practices and beliefs that their philosophy denied? Perhaps. But one does not sense the kind of almost conspiratorial estrangement from politics and society on the part of philosophers in ancient China that has been described for classical philosophy in the West.* Yet there was one fundamental difference in

---

* Allan Bloom. *The Closing of the American Mind.* New York: Simon & Schuster, 1987. Especially "The Relation between Thought and Civil Society" and "The Philosophical Experience," pp. 256–284.

the way the world was managed in ancient China. Categorizing "heresies" and combating "dangerous cults" in that world of harmonious process also occurred, but it was done in ways only superficially analogous to the way such problems were managed in, for example, the world of premodern Christendom. In Christendom as in other societies dominated by revealed religions, the imperative for combating heresies and dangerous cults could draw upon religion's nonrational sources of authority. In China the justifications for such action might reflect the state's interests or the norms of social practice as maintained by local elites, neither of which was necessarily reasonable. Or they could enlist the reasoning minds of philosophers (and scholar-officials educated in philosophy in later imperial times) although philosophers' distance from political action, there as elsewhere, allowed them little direct involvement. Regardless of what forces were used to manage dissidence, the important difference in the Chinese case is that neither political regimes nor social leaders intent on quelling deviant thought and behavior, nor the philosophers and guardians of the high tradition, could claim to represent the exclusive truths of revealed religion. That conditioned attitudes and modes of behavior. A more thoughtful consideration of the ways in which the Chinese world view affected all aspects of society will help us understand China.

TIME-SPACE CONCEPTS   Of great interest is the problem of time concepts or of time-space concepts. The word for cosmology in Chinese is *yü-chou-kuan,* or the "concept of *yü* and *chou.*" These two syllables literally mean "eaves" and "ridgepole," parts of a roof, or the boundary markers of a known kind of enclosed space. But they also have very early explanations, going all the way back to the fourth century B.C. and the text of the *Chuang Tzu,* of the separate ideas of time and space. The cosmos thus is explained in terms of people's awareness of their place in time and space. Needham compares early Chinese thought to what he calls the Whiteheadian preference for reticular relationship, or "process," whereas Western thought has been deeply influenced by the Newtonian preference for "particulate, catenary" causal explanation; that is, Whitehead describes the cosmic process as a netlike interweaving of events, while Newton conceives of it as a series of discrete events linked in a causal chain. The cosmic process, the Chinese felt, in a many-sided fashion affects one's life within it, because each person is an active element in that process.

This cosmology made necessary two kinds of time. One was cyclic cosmic time, with no beginning point, no Year One. Stages of cosmic "process" (for example, the generative process of the self-contained cosmos itself) were seen as a set of logical, not chronological, relationships. The cosmic process is one in which all stages are simultaneously present. The other kind of time, however, was the developmental, linear time of human history, in which human cumulative achievement in devising culture had its beginning point, suggested if not precisely known.

History, culture, and people's conceptions of their ideal roles all must be explained in terms of Chinese cosmology, and not—if we really want to understand Chinese civilization—by implicit analogy to ours. It is not too much to suggest that an ill-detected cosmological gulf separates Western civilization, as well as other civilizations including Eastern ones, from Chinese civilization. Hence the records of Chinese culture must be interpreted, and the texts translated and retranslated until our inadvertent uses of historical and cultural analogy are detected, weighed, and, if necessary, corrected. It is somewhat awesome to realize that this is a task the Chinese also have to perform, for the mirror images of these same problems of interpretation of our culture in terms of theirs also exist for them to grapple with.

We may speculate that all national cultural peculiarities and identities will tend to diminish and even disappear in the future, as science provides us not only with increasingly uniform technologies, but also with a new universal (as all things in science must strive to be) cosmogony and cosmology. In fact the cleavages within societies in which a science-oriented elite coexists with a mass population still tied to religiously derived cosmologies, as in our own society, may be greater than any difference between traditional China on its side of the cosmological gulf and our civilization on this side of it. But science cannot be expected to homogenize all cultures rapidly enough for us to be spared the trouble of understanding those different from our own. We must first of all be ready to conceive of and prepared to observe the most essential and consequential differences.

Chapter Three
Early Confucianism

Confucius, so far as we know, never called himself a *ju* (pronounced like "rue"), but he advised his disciples to be "genuine *ju*," and later Confucian usage so fixed the word throughout the post-Confucian millennia of Chinese history that *ju* is best translated as "Confucian" or sometimes more loosely as "an educated man." To understand Confucius' place in Chinese history, we must know what the word had meant before his time, if indeed it was a word in general currency at all in early Chou times. The explanation that has become most influential says that the word has the basic semantic value of "weak" or "yielding." It was applied to the learned aristocracy of the Shang court who, after the conquest by the martial Chou dynasty, had to serve new overlords as compliant, subservient experts on the ritual and the techniques of government. In contrast with the self-confident knights (*shih*) of the Chou, the *ju* of the Shang were a powerless group who were aware of their intellectual superiority, but were still willing to perpetuate their literate high culture because of their devotion to its intrinsic values and use it in the service of the new dynasty. Their learning made them indispensable to the Chou; at the same time it was vital to the *ju* in their struggle to maintain status and importance. It is not surprising that they revered their traditions and prized their command of the technical knowledge of their time so highly. Nor is it unexpected that out of their traditions should come a school of thought which would have these features as its hallmarks.

The Ju Tradition

It is perhaps possible to see the *ju* tradition as the heir to still earlier and more primitive traditions of shamanism. Shamans, divinely touched holy men and women who could communicate with gods and spirits and advise kings and chieftains about the conduct of life, have existed in many of the cultures on the periphery of the Chinese high culture area, especially in Inner Asia to the north. They were also important in the Ch'u culture of the Yangtze Valley, the chief competitor of the North Chinese Shang and Chou cultures until late in the first millennium B.C., when the Ch'u culture area finally was absorbed into the central Chinese cultural world. Some traces of shamanism are apparent in some regional subcultures of China until considerably later—in fact, until today. It would be convenient to regard the *ju* as the transformed, rationalized shamans of the Great Tradition in the central culture, but we have no evidence for so simple a solution. We do not even have explicit evidence for referring to the learned group of political advisors and ritual experts as *ju* throughout the Shang and early Chou periods, but let us for simplicity's sake do so here.

We can say that Shang culture had become a "wise man," rather than a "holy man," culture, and with the increasingly rational tone of early Chou times, the group of expert government advisors and assistants came to play a greater and more influential role in the life of the state and of society at large. Perhaps in late Shang times they were still principally advisors on the spirit world and on a person's formalized behavior in those ritual situations in which he or she was supposed to act in ways analogous to those of the spirit world. Not all societies develop so extensively and consciously formalized behavior as did the Chinese, and the religious beliefs of antiquity are at the base of their ritualized secular life. But already in Shang times the justification for ritual is only semireligious; the harmony of the human and the spirit spheres of life began to have secular ethical meaning, and the source of the authority for ritualized behavior gradually was transferred from the superrational to a purely rational plane. The models for it, undoubtedly magical and drawn from the spirit world in early Shang, became pseudohistorical. Sage-kings, still to be sure possessing some religious character, displaced spirits as the sources of knowledge about government and society, and their accumulated wisdom was recorded in books and archives that people could interpret rationally. The wise man's command of written records had replaced the holy man's ability to summon the spirits.

Ritual came to be philosophically conceived as something that contributed to the harmony of the cosmos. The sage-kings had prescribed it because they knew it helped maintain harmony. The *ju* had access to what the sages had prescribed, for they could read and record, and they could perform divinations and interpret the results according to the great book of divination, the I Ching, to which they never ascribed any character of revealed truth, of arbitrary commandment, or of superrational binding authority. Reasonableness gradually replaced arbitrary authority.

The functions the *ju* had acquired in pre-Confucian times are those which in other societies might have been performed by priests. In Chou China these functions lacked the sanction of religion and the instrument of an organized church, but they acquired a mystique of legitimacy and propriety that made them equally, though not similarly, authoritative. Among the functions of the *ju* were these: First they ordered the ceremonial relations with the spirits of the ancestors—especially the ancestors of the Chou rulers, the enfiefed heads of the ducal houses, and others possessing political legitimacy derived from the Chou kings. Since the Chou Mandate from Heaven to rule the people was held by the clan and involved responsibility to the royal ancestors, and since most of the ducal fiefs were held by clan relatives, political authority within the Chou hegemony was inextricably involved with the clan ancestral cult. Second, they observed astronomical phenomena in order to understand the seasons and to adjust and proclaim the calendar. The calendar was the supreme royal prerogative; failure to acknowledge and use it was treason. But at the same time, if its beginnings and its seasons were not correct, that was evidence of disharmony between the ruler and nature and proof of failure that could threaten the Mandate. Indeed it did threaten the dynasty simply by reason of being a prodigious occurrence. Thus the *ju* had to make expert astronomical observations and calculations that required the keeping of detailed and accurate records. From the office of astronomer emerged that of the historian. Third, as the literate men of the courts, the *ju* commanded historical data, knowledge of precedents, and the recorded wisdom of their predecessors. Thus they filled the purely bureaucratic functions of recorders, advisors, and technical experts on government. In all the roles of the *ju*, it was their wisdom and their command of specialized book learning that gave them their competence.

In Shang times this learned group at the court had been hereditary aristocrats. After the Chou conquest they filled roles that must have been frustrating for ambitious men, and they must have been tempted to think seditiously about the return of the Mandate to the Shang house. Confucius, who was descended from the Shang remnants still self-consciously aware of the conflicting Shang-versus-Chou demands on loyalty six hundred years after the Chou conquest, gives the credit for devising a basis for Shang-Chou common interest and cooperation to the great Duke of Chou (twelfth century B.C.). This paragon also was a son of King Wen, a younger brother of the conqueror, King Wu, and regent to Wu's son and successor, King Ch'eng. Some modern historians have argued that the Duke of Chou is at best a shadowy figure in ancient history. Yet to Confucius he was the luminous figure of the great philosopher-statesman, surest evidence that the Mandate of Heaven had truly passed to the Chou house and symbol of the amalgamation of the Shang and Chou cultures. Perhaps it was one of Confucius' most creative achievements to have made so meaningful a reconstruction of a historical and cultural symbol. However he might have misconceived the history of the past, he created one of the most important elements in China's subsequent history. Although a descendant of the Shang, Confucius' political slogan was: I follow the Chou. Confucius became, in the period when Chou real power had long since eroded and when disturbing social and cultural change threatened the stability of Chou life, the greatest defender of the Chou political order. At the same time, he rallied the intellectual leadership of China to the Chou cause in a way that had enduring results in the life of Chinese culture and virtually no enduring significance in politics. The Chou political structure continued to crumble, and then disappeared. "I follow Chou" was more than a political slogan; it was a statement of cultural policy. Thereafter Chou cultural and intellectual values, enlarged and universalized by Confucius, channeled the mainstream of Chinese life.

How could Confucius, a mere *ju* in an age of political turmoil, who had no resources other than expert command of the high traditions of Chinese culture, accomplish so much? There is no other founding figure quite like him in any of the world's national histories.

Confucius

The prosperity of the Chou dynasty ended with a barbarian invasion from Inner Asia from 771 to 770 B.C. The Chou kings then were forced to move their capital eastward to modern Loyang on the Yellow River, and the Royal Chou state was thereafter no more than a tiny principality surrounded by a decreasing number of larger and more powerful feudatories. Though in fact independent kingdoms, they long continued to acknowledge Chou suzerainty. Chou society had become totally civilized, that is, demilitarized. Chou power had become totally ritualized—a mystique of power had supplanted real power. The ju tradition had contributed greatly to both these developments.

As Chou society was progressively demilitarized, the ju as the wielders of its civil instruments became more important than the increasingly obsolete class of knights (shih). The shih, the lowest rank in the Chou hereditary aristocracy, originally the most competitive with and most hostile to the ju, now tended to merge with them. When (before and after the time of Confucius) changes in military technology—gradual obsolescence of chariot warfare, rise of mass conscription armies, and introduction of cavalry—totally eliminated the military functions of the old knightly class, they were able to identify so closely with the ju tradition and functions that ju and shih became words of the same meaning; in later Chinese usage, either can be translated "scholar," and shih especially came to mean simply "scholar-official."

Just as the knights had been the guardians of the original Chou military power, so the ju from mid-Chou times onward became the guardians of the mystique of Chou legitimacy which in functional terms replaced real military power. As guardians of the traditions on which that mystique of power rested, the ju manipulated the expert knowledge needed to retain Chou prerogatives so successfully that the dynasty lasted another five hundred years. This remarkable prolongation until 256 B.C. is certain evidence of the ju success in manipulating the symbols of legitimacy and keeping them meaningful long after they had ceased to warrant such meaning in a "real power" sense.

Confucius, although a self-proclaimed man of Shang descent and professionally a man of books and learning, also had much of the forthright character of the Chou fighting knight. He was heir to both aspects of the *ju/shih* mentality, evidence that the two groups were in fact becoming one social group with a single identity. One consequence of his life work was to complete the amalgamation process by providing the new universalized ideal of the "superior man" with a coherent ideological ground that retained all the inner tensions between the two ideal types from which it derived. The time in which Confucius lived was a watershed of history, a turbulent time of rapid growth and consequent dislocation, when divisive but vital changes occurred. In such a time the opportunities for a creative response to the unusual strains and pulls tended to produce reflective, systematic thinking about human problems—or philosophy—and the peculiar risks of public life tended to urge the even marginally meditative toward the reflective life.

Confucius (551–479 B.C.) was the first self-conscious philosopher in the Chinese tradition of whom we are aware. He was soon followed by a large number of others who differed from his philosophic stand in greater or less degree and who developed a whole spectrum of thought and of programs for the times. Confucius and his school dominated one end of the spectrum, the end characterized by social conservatism and a nostalgia for the past. Most of all the Confucian school was characterized by its strong ethical sense, its social responsibility, and its constructive, rational approach to immediate problems.

In socioeconomic terms the period from the sixth to the third centuries B.C. was a burgeoning time. Iron had already come into general use for making agricultural implements and weapons; agricultural yields were considerably increased by this and other technological changes. Peasants, up to mid-Chou times largely bound to the soil like medieval European serfs, were becoming free landowning farmers. Surnames were becoming fixed possessions of all members of society about fifteen hundred years earlier than in any other society in history. The old aristocracy was losing its prerogatives, especially those of automatic right to officeholding in the national and local governments. There were new and great opportunities for upward mobility:

The competition among the states to succeed in economic development, warfare, and diplomacy offered a broad market for talent, a
market that was not stuffy about social background. States that could
modernize quickly by developing entrepreneurial and industrial mo-
nopolies and by creating more efficient political forms could expand
at their neighbors' expense. Immorality in public life, boisterous disregard for the time-honored values of the stable old order, increasing
physical hazards as warfare became more frequent and more deadly,
all these familiar-sounding by-products of change dismayed Confucius.
Yet he did not have much at stake in the old order in any material
sense, and he did not respond in a hidebound way. On the contrary,
whether he knew it or not, the long-range implication of his response
to this situation is that he created the ideological foundations for the
emerging new society, a society which he can scarcely have anticipated
and probably would not have found congenial. It is for this reason that
modern scholars have debated whether he was a reactionary or a
revolutionary, a mere transmitter of values (as he called himself) or a
practical social reformer.

Confucius was born in 551 B.C. in the southwestern part of the
modern province of Shantung, in what at that time was the state of
Lu. His surname was K'ung, his name Ch'iu. Fu-tzu added following
his surname is an honorific equivalent to saying "the Master Philosopher K'ung." This form, K'ung Fu-tzu, was Latinized by sixteenth- and
seventeenth-century Europeans as Confucius.

The state of Lu had been the fief of the duke of Chou; it cherished
the highest cultural traditions and prided itself on its authentic links
to the great age of the Chou dynasty. Confucius' grandfather had fled
to Chou from the state of Sung that is associated with the Shang
descendants. There the family had enjoyed some minor eminence in
the nobility, but in the state of Lu they were fallen aristocracy, victims
of the political uncertainty and social mobility that characterized the
age.

Confucius was ambitious to make a career by his own efforts in the
public world of government. But he was not really suited to the cour-
tier life, which in that age demanded a willingness to engage in flattery
and to attach oneself to a powerful figure and assist him in the unprin-
cipled exercise of power. Confucius was too frank and too fussy for
such a life. He was a troublesome person to have around. Unyielding
in his principles and the most learned man of his time, he could invoke

great knowledge in support of those principles. As a minor hanger-on at the Lu court, he sought more important office for some years, then for a decade wandered through the neighboring states throughout North China hoping to find an enlightened ruler in some other state who would heed his advice.

In 484, a disappointed old man, he returned to Lu; five years later he died there. He had achieved nothing by which he himself or his contemporaries could count him a success. One of his students once asked him how he should be described, and his answer is his best epitaph: "He is this sort of man: so intent upon enlightening those eager for knowledge that he forgets to eat, and so happy in doing so that he forgets his sorrows, and does not realize that old age is creeping up on him."*

This is an unpretentious man's evaluation of himself. It fails, probably intentionally, to indicate the great originality of the man and the scope of his achievement. Confucius chose to designate himself a "mere transmitter" of antique learning, but in fact he must be credited with three innovations that remained permanent features of Chinese civilization, at least until virtually today. These three, together with the body of thought that in China came to be called the learning of the *ju*, and which we call Confucianism, are important among what we regard as the defining characteristics of Chinese civilization. No one did more to impart enduring shape and character to a civilization than Confucius.

His first innovation is the creation of the role of the private teacher. Confucius was a lifelong scholar, and his times already honored learning as something functionally significant for the public good. Despite this, Chou society had devised no institution for transmitting learning other than on-the-job training for expectant officials or junior officials in their first posts. Such persons came automatically to these posts as a prerogative of their birth, having presumably had some basic literacy training in their homes. But there were no professional teachers and no schools as such. Confucius slid into the role of the first professional teacher no doubt without quite realizing it. As the most learned man at the court of Lu, although of inconsequential office, he was regularly consulted by others, and he extended the teaching role

* *The Analects* 7/18.

gradually so that it became his main activity instead of an incidental one. He must have been so good at it that the activity grew of itself.

He taught as an expectant official for forty years, marking time until he would take up the real work of his life. But after returning from his decade of wanderings, he undoubtedly realized that the "real work" would never come and that teaching had become his true vocation. Yet because he never really quite abandoned his fervent hope of doing something more, he could not teach with total detachment. His instruction retained its practical orientation. And in the lively sense of involvement in the world's real concerns, he established the pattern of student-teacher relations and the model of the professional teacher so effectively that they quickly became standard throughout the society and were never challenged by any subsequent competing models.

His second innovation is closely related to the first: Together they help explain the significance and the permanence of each. He created and established the content of education and its methods and ideals. Although education was quite specifically for one kind of career—that of public service—Confucius believed in the broad liberal arts learning. It included study of certain venerated books, especially the Odes, the Book of Documents, and the ritual texts. These were studied both philologically and as applied philosophy; that is, the study of them involved not only language and literature, but also history and ethics. Above all the emphasis was on the right way of government. Studies were supplemented by music and athletics. This unspecialized, non-professional education, not unlike that which English gentlemen acquired in the eighteenth and nineteenth centuries in preparation for governing the British Empire, remained the education that all men of learning would receive for the next two and one-half millennia in China. Men so educated have been expected to meet any need that public life might bring—quell rebellion, build canals, devise fiscal measures, record the histories of their times. Until very recently, when government had to begin to meet the more complex needs of modernizing societies, this education sufficed. It had no inherent shortcomings that it could not correct. Moreover, being a rational and open-minded kind of education, it could grow with the constantly growing and developing civilization without becoming sterile and rigid. Confucius in his own lifetime established the texts that form the core of this education, established the method of teaching them, and defined the ideal standard by which to measure a person's progress.

Confucian teachings were transmitted faithfully, yet were received in ever-changing settings over the passage of centuries. The intellectual content of pristine Confucianism, nonetheless, was always recoverable in later ages by the very methods that Confucius taught—careful study of the texts. Throughout Chinese history reform characteristically took the form of going back to the ancients to correct current practices and misinterpretations. Everyone had the right and the responsibility to become an authority on how Confucian teachings and all the classical texts should be understood and applied. While any would-be reformer might impute, correctly or not, sincerely or not, "authority" to those ancient voices, the only real authority in their interpretation came from the quality of mind and learning with which interpretations of the past were put forth.

The third innovation, and the most difficult of the three to assess and explain, is that Confucius accepted students of all social backgrounds and clearly established the principle for doing so. Of his several dozens of students about whom we know enough to identify them adequately as historical personages, only two were from the aristocracy. All the others were commoners, many of quite humble background. Though Confucius, it must be stressed, longed for a return to the standards of the good old days when a closed society had existed, he permanently destroyed the privilege crucial to the maintenance of that society, the privilege of automatic entry into office. "Princelings" (chün-tzu) or sons of aristocrats alone had been eligible for legally privileged status and office. Confucius insisted that the name chün-tzu should apply only to those "superior men" who gave evidence of having achieved a personal superiority of ethical and intellectual cultivation, and that it should then apply to any man who could give such evidence. This revolutionary redefinition of the criterion for assigning status in society was formulated at a time when the old criterion was becoming obsolete anyway, and it can be argued that Confucius' purpose was to revitalize the old aristocracy by challenging its members to buck up and play their proper parts. But the evidence that he openly invited men of all backgrounds and classes to be his students in order to become "superior men" and that he proclaimed this as the proper standard for education forces us to interpret Confucius' intent differently. It does not, of course, prove that he understood and intended the social evolution that drew its ideological support from this very teaching. China's society found in Confucius' teachings the mechanism for regulating and for encouraging social mobility as well as the essential justification for the ideal of an open society. Did *he* know what he was doing? This is the disputable point that has provided so much ground for debate, especially in contemporary China.

In reflecting upon Confucius' achievement as a teacher, we must ask how it was that such a man, doing something that seems so natural a development for that civilization and that time, could nonetheless achieve something so genuinely new. The significant element seems to have been the force of his own personality. Let us assume that the rationalization of the educational procedures would have occurred anyway and that the breakdown of the old aristocratic system would have been acknowledged sooner or later. The range of possibilities for meeting these needs was considerable; the chance of quickly achieving a lasting and functionally adequate solution was not very great. Yet both occurred. And they would not have occurred in that way had not Confucius been a man of particular insight, capable of advancing solutions that were both deeply perceptive and convincing. Confucius clearly had a prepossessing personality. He was capable of communicating great enthusiasm for the nobility of his ideas along with the belief that they were applicable to the world's needs. And his ideas did possess great breadth. They were altruistically universal, yet not vapid. People sought him because he really did possess the most accurate currently available understanding of his civilization and how it ideally should work. In his learning-oriented civilization, such understanding counted for a great deal. At the same time, his education brought practical results. It became known that his students were a cut above the ordinary job seekers, and that made them eminently employable. Although Confucius never got his own coveted prime ministership, many of his students advanced rapidly in government. Within a few generations the students of his widely proliferated school commanded the market—they had the talent, they got the positions.

Yet Confucius denounced certain bright and unscrupulous students who used their education to get ahead, but in so doing forgot the moral responsibilities he considered essential to the "superior man." And this points to another explanation of his achievements. The tyrants and the politicians put up with Confucius because, despite his troublesome insistence on norms and standards, he was trustworthy. The chaotic times made a man of integrity especially valuable, and Confucius' followers were indoctrinated in loyalty and integrity above all. Moreover he taught reform by moral suasion, not by revolution. His students did not become immediate dangers to the established order in any of the obvious ways. Hence they were apparently less dangerous than others. In addition they could be counted on to possess skills that were truly useful in that society. So the rulers of the time, even those who did not merit the sage's personal approval and who knew it, nonetheless actively cultivated his students.

If the intimate awareness of Confucius the man has been forcefully conveyed to each of the eighty generations in the almost twenty-five hundred years since his death as each successive age has cut its teeth on his *Analects*, Confucius the philosopher is harder for us to apprehend. The ideas themselves are not abstruse, but the system of ideas does not emerge as a formal structure of the kind the West demands of any philosophy. We suspect that the core of Confucian thought lacks structure and formal design, for the works that record the sage's ideas do not present them in that fashion. And indeed, there is no reason to believe that, either in its concerns or in its methods, the early history of Chinese philosophy closely paralleled that of the classical Greek world; so if formal philosophy is to be defined by the standards we have inherited from the Greeks, then early China did not have any.

Even if so parochial a standard is eschewed, there are real problems in reconstructing a systematic thought for Confucius and many other early Chinese thinkers. Confucius was groping to find precise language tools for expressing his ideas. He apparently was the first reflective, systematic thinker (since we have adopted that simple definition for philosopher) in the Chinese tradition. Words had not yet acquired the technical, particularized, rigorous meanings that philosophers need in order to use them for purposes lying so far beyond ordinary day-to-day uses. In his thinking about the ethical problems of society and government, Confucius was trying to universalize certain heretofore specific and limited words like *chün-tzu* ("princeling" with specific reference to the old aristocratic social order, but now coming to mean the "superior man" in a universal sense) and *jen* ("goodness" or "benevolence," perhaps derived from its homonym meaning "human," and now enlarged to mean "humane"). He found it difficult to articulate definitions of such terms and tried to show from devised situations and anecdotes what he thought these terms should now mean in the context of his philosophical views. This problem of language, of emergent philosophical jargon, is one of the reasons we have trouble reconstructing the system of Confucius' thought.

Another problem for us is that the thrust of his thought was practical and ethical rather than theoretical and metaphysical. Hence he tended to verify his ideas by discussions of concrete problems, especially historical ones, rather than by creating abstract or highly generalized statements. A third problem (formerly considered fatal by Western students of comparative philosophy) is that the Chinese did not develop any precise formula like the syllogism for measuring the validity of statements. Modern students of formal logic can read most of the logical patterns now known, such as those utilizing the logic of terms, the logic of categories or classes, and so forth, into the arguments of the Chinese sophists in particular. But the Chinese did not analyze the patterns or make formulas of them the way the Greeks did; they attached less value to systems and structures of ideas. We cannot say for sure that the validity of their statements existed in their eyes because formal tests of their validity were consciously employed, even when our analysis of their arguments shows that they in fact pass our tests. In any event, Confucius and his school disdained highly developed formal argumentation as misleading and useless, preferring to construct arguments based on chains of contingencies, or upon implicit appeals to a self-evident reasonableness, or upon the authority of a manifestly superior ethical system of wide acceptance at the base of which was the Chinese family structure.

And finally the system of Confucian thought is hard to reconstruct because Confucius is recorded for us only in brief and random statements. If he engaged in sustained philosophical argument, we have no way of knowing it, for no essays from his pen exist, if indeed any were even written. His followers in the first and second generation after his death made up a collection of what had survived as his most memorable pronouncements, and this became The Analects (Lun Yü). Much of it reads like punch lines of anecdotes or arguments now deprived of their linguistic as well as their social context. Not until we come to Mencius, and even better to Hsün Tzu, do we have any examples of sustained Confucian philosophical argument designed to be read as discourse on philosophical topics. But from The Analects and from the impression that Confucius' teachings made on the next generation or two of his followers, we can take those ideas that were stressed and reconstruct, if not a systematic philosophy, a coherent set of intellectual concerns.

Within that set of intellectual concerns, the element that counts for the most is no doubt the ethical one. Confucius was convinced that the cosmos is a moral order and that human affairs can prosper only when they are in harmony with the moral nature of the world. The remarkable feature of this, of course, is that the foundations of Confucius' ethical system are secular; his moral principles derive no authority from supernatural revelation but are simply the self-justifying, obviously reasonable discoveries of sages and worthies of the historical past. Even if we now determine that it was an encapsulated and somewhat pseudohistorical past, it had the character of a rationally known epoch of normal human experience. There is some sense of cosmic retribution in all early Chinese thought, but it is not mechanical or specific in its operation in the sense that a particular bad deed brings inevitably a particular punishment or a good deed a measured reward. Evil action tends to break down the structure of heaven and earth, but generally, and not as a specific threat, opening a specific breach. The general good of the family and of society is the primary reason for adhering to the principles of ethical conduct. They are merely principles, not precise regulations; individual acts are always to be assessed in relation to particular circumstances in the spirit of "suspended judgment." Everything in the Confucian world resists legalistically codified and objectified norms; for binding legal codes it substitutes basic principles which wise and humane citizens, considering all the particular circumstances of each case, can humanly apply.

Confucius fully accepted the ethics of a family-centered society. The individual's primary duty was to the family, and the grades of responsibility lessened as one went beyond the family to the extended clan, to the village or community, to the state, and finally to the whole of human society, uniting it harmoniously with heaven or the cosmic order. Politics to Confucius was merely the extension of ethics to the larger society. Filial submission (hsiao) was the primary virtue; loyalty to the state and its leader (chung) never could become more than the second most important ethical principle, even when later the essentially non-Confucian imperial state adapted Confucian doctrines to its needs. Most of the sayings in The Analects have ethical relevance, and the absolute primacy of humanistic ethics in a human-centered world may be taken as the ultimate touchstone of Confucianism. When later scholars argue that Hsün Tzu was "Legalistic" or that the Han dynasty thinker Wang Ch'ung was "Taoistic," we need only apply this fundamental measure to determine that they were Confucians after all.

It is a non sequitur frequently indulged in by modern-minded writers to state that, since Confucius had a secular foundation adequate for his ethical system, he therefore was wholly irreligious or, by extension, that religion is therefore irrelevant to Confucian civilization. True enough, Confucius unequivocally declared religious issues to be irrelevant to his teachings; he answered the famous question about death and the spirits by saying that since we cannot know fully about humankind and this life, we need not bother ourselves about death and the spirits. This makes it clear that this life here and now is of primary importance to people here and now, but that is not the same as if Confucius had expostulated "Sheer rubbish!" on hearing the question. And in telling people how to participate in the family and state sacrifices, he cautions that they should assume a spirit of reverence "As if the spirits were present." "As if" may mean that they are not, or that they may not always be, or that he does not know, but the attitude of reverence is appropriate in any case.

The system of family-centered worship of or respect to ancestors was already long established by his time, as were many features of popular religion and the state cults. Confucius accepted these and left it to each individual to make of them what he could or would. Throughout the subsequent millennia, Confucian learning remained a set of teachings that could accommodate to many religions without conflict. Ultimately the Confucian tradition encountered the exclusive religions of the Judeo-Christian-Islamic tradition; all fully understanding believers of these religions in China have had to surrender some points of their Confucian tradition. But most Chinese have had considerable resistance to exclusive systems of belief.

The rewards of the ethical life Confucius urged upon all people were quite in keeping with the old traditions of his civilization. He created no new conception of some paradise here or elsewhere, though he did attempt to revitalize the belief that human civilization was capable of recapturing a Golden Age of peace and plenty. Ancient Shang and Chou bronze vessels cast to commemorate the enfiefment of a feudal lord or for use as sacrificial vessels on the family altar characteristically bore the sentiments "to honor my ancestors" and "to feast my friends." Confucius accepted those ideals.

People were not to be ethical for the sake of going to heaven or saving their souls, or even for some mechanical reward which the vague sense of moral retribution could not guarantee anyone. Instead people were ethical because it was their nature to be so. Also it was practical; it contributed to a better life for all. But even if being ethical got someone in trouble, a right-thinking person would do it for its own sake, for the sense of satisfaction that it brings. Such a person also tried to be a moral paragon for the kind of immortality it would bring to his or her memory and the good will it would gain for the clan and family.

Such an ethical system grants each individual a highly personal satisfaction in heeding its standards but directs every person's behavior toward the good of the family and the larger society. Taoism and later on Buddhism, with their egocentric individualism, seemed to the Confucians to be the very epitome of personal selfishness, because they lacked the ethical sense that should be humanity's distinguishing characteristic.

The primary virtue Confucius urged on his followers for their personal cultivation, and the quality that more than any other defined the "superior man" for him, is jen. This has been translated as "benevolence," as "love," as "goodness," as "human heartedness," all with some justification. Like all the Confucian virtues, to Confucians it seems to lack meaning unless practiced; and the practice of jen requires everyone to express concern for the well-being of others. It also demands an attitude of humane understanding for all human conditions. The ideal of government is a government of jen, one that so cares for the basic needs of society that it will not have to use coercion in order to maintain social order. Confucius was a theoretician of government, never a governor. Later Confucians bearing responsibilities for governing often felt the rightness of this vague ideal so strongly that they struggled to realize it in practice and characteristically blamed themselves when they could not.

The other Confucian virtues are also virtues of action. Second in importance to jen is chih or "intelligence" (often translated "wisdom"). This meant to Confucians not merely the possession of knowledge, but especially the integrating mind, the ability to know correct action and to follow it. Confucian thought stressed the necessity for everyone to know by and of themselves, to make their own judgments rather than vindicate laws—hence the importance of wisely informed intelligence.

And a third virtue, demanded by the responsibility of all persons to make their own essential judgments about what action is right in any set of circumstances, is *yung* or "courage."

There is a list of further virtues, all qualities we might expect to follow from these three: trustworthiness, a sense of shame, altruism, and so forth. The only virtue quite peculiar to the Chinese cultural scene, and one which induced problems of emphasis and interpretation for later Confucians, is that of *li* or a sense of ritual correctness, usually translated "propriety." There is an obvious tension between the personal expression of the commiserating heart or *jen*, and the adherence to social norms implicit in *li*. The partiality to one of these at the expense of the other accounts for, or exposes, part of the disagreement between Mencius and Hsün Tzu and remains symbolic of the tensions within Confucian thought.

Confucian political thought turns on the search for order in a turbulent world. It asks the question: Where does the well-ordered society begin? And typically not only for Confucian thought but for the whole intellectual world of ancient China, the answer dwells on human psychology. To achieve the perfect society you must begin with the individual. The human mind is the only instrument for effecting change. A text dating from the century after Confucius, which claims to be quoting Confucius and which has remained of central importance to the Confucian school, contains a passage that makes explicit the link between the individual human mind and the problems of government.

> To be fond of learning is to draw close to *chih* (wisdom). To practice with vigor is to draw close to *jen* (benevolence). To know the sense of shame is to draw close to *yung* (courage). He who knows these three things knows how to cultivate his own character. Knowing how to cultivate his own character, he knows how to govern other men. Knowing how to govern other men, he knows how to govern the world, its states and its families.*

Similarly in the *Great Learning* (vi), another text of like provenance, Confucius is made to say: "From the Son of Heaven [the head of the

---

* *The Doctrine of the Mean*, xx/10–11, slightly modified, in *Chinese Classics*, James Legge, trans. 5 vols. HongKong: University of HongKong Press, 1960, vol. 1, p. 407.

state] down to the mass of the people, all must consider the cultivation of the person as the root of everything besides."* The idea is repeatedly encountered throughout the Confucian writings: Civilization is humankind's greatest achievement, it is of our own human making, and the human mind alone is able to affect it for the better or the worse.

This emphasis on human psychology and the perceptive observation of psychological factors almost justifies the view that Chinese philosophy in general is a philosophy of human psychology. Moreover, in the Confucian scheme of things especially, the psyche is held to be sensitive to moral influences. Hence self-cultivation on an individual basis means coming under the moral force of the great sage-like models, and government at its best is likewise government by moral suasion. The state ideally does not coerce, it leads; the ruler is like the wind, and the people bend to his influence like the grass. Thus it follows that government is of men, not of laws. There is strong distrust of laws as something inviting people to be tricky, bringing out the worst in them; whereas good governors exerting the personal influence of their moral force bring out the best in men. The state, of course, needs some general codes as manifestations of its standards, but administration of government can never be one of rigid enforcement of the laws which, in any case, can never be so meaningful to the people as the good example set by their rulers and governors. A king who must rely on laws and their forceful application is thus by definition morally deficient. Confucianism adopted an antilegalistic, wholly humanistic attitude toward government, thanks to Confucius and to Mencius, who also never had to assume administrative responsibility. Hsün Tzu, who did, tried to maintain the ideal while modifying it to the realities of office.

Confucians' suspicions of laws is understandable; they saw laws as essentially punitive instruments for regularizing behavior and as evidence of administrators' unthinking avoidance of their primary obligation to teach and to provide suasive moral example. But modern scholars have seen in that distrust of laws the source of Chinese political weakness throughout the imperial era into modern times. Laws in that setting had no way of becoming transcendent Law, or

---

* Legge, *Chinese Classics*, vol. 1, p. 359.

government becoming a Government of Law, in which lawfulness was
something noble and inviolable, with laws binding on all alike and
embodying impersonal standards of justice. Instead laws remained
mere instruments of the state, could be changed to suit rulers' conve-
nience, and could be evaded without great moral cost. Such were
Confucians' criticisms of the later Legalists (discussed in Chapter 7),
and they were not unjustified criticisms. There seems to be no way that
China's civilization would have generated a sense of law as a system
of rights and obligations having its own moral force, the way the
Greeks, especially Aristotle, analyzed the idea of law philosophically.
In any event, that did not happen.

One need not blame the Confucians for that. It is more realistic
to say that given the absence of preconditions for such a development,
Confucius and his followers struggled to make of the ethical norms,
and of their intense social consciousness, a force that would protect
society's and the individual's interests. Beyond that they expected that
refined institutions, a major focus of their attention as historians and
as scholar-officials, would support the altruistic spirit of good government.

Confucius' methods in governing involved two central intellectual
preoccupations. One is that of the correspondence of name and reality. He expressed this as the need to *cheng ming* or "rectify the names."
A discrepancy between name and reality was to him evidence of breakdown at the top. "A world without order" was the result. A name
implied content; when that was lacking, it was evidence of a human
deficiency. Herein lay the political method. Restore the content, and
thereby restore order.

To restore the content, make the deficient individual in question
aware of the discrepancy in a way that arouses his sense of shame, and
thereby influence him morally and intellectually to correct the situation. That is, the name "king" implies the content of one who is
morally worthy and politically effective because his words and deeds
are all kingly. To call him a king when he is not one in that sense is
to perpetuate the discrepancy. Remind him of it, and he will or should
strive to be king-like. His servitors will then be influenced to be true
ministers. So must fathers really be what the word implies, else they
do not merit the name. And when they merit it, their sons will be true
sons. When these four names, king, minister, father, and son, can be
applied to a whole society with no inappropriateness, perfect order in

society and the state will exist. Altering names was intended to correct realities.

Confucius did not go about calling people by names that were analytically more fitting; he still addressed the kings of his time as kings—and none of them deserved the name. His method was the more subtle one of using history for didactic purposes. The written word was essential for effecting social improvement; the use of words became subject to the most subtle considerations. Whether the commentaries on the classics and the editing of the annals of the state of Lu, as we now know them, come directly from him is difficult to establish, but the tradition of using these works primarily for the didactic purpose of pointing up discrepancies between name and reality clearly stems from his example. It remained a preoccupation of the Confucian tradition, having the questionable consequence of interfering with the appreciation of literary values for their own sake, but no doubt making the record of the past supremely important as a subject of study and thereby helping to preserve it. The Chinese historical experience is by far the most extensively documented one in all human history, even though it fails to record all the aspects of society that modern scholars wish to know about. The Confucian mainstream of later Chinese intellectual life took the lesson of history very seriously; history functioned as revelation did in other civilizations.

The second method of government in Confucius' thought is that of first nurturing, then teaching, and only last governing. Confucianism was quite realistic about the material basis of ethics; hungry people cannot be expected to be good. Therefore the state must in the first instance provide the basic livelihood and not take excessively or waste. That condition satisfied, government can then transform its citizens through correct example and teaching. Only after teaching has been established need it concern itself with tasks of directly governing, and those should be of limited scope and should not become burdensome to the governed.

Despite this orientation Confucians really believed in government. They felt called to serve and regarded no other activity as of equal value. They were activists, always challenged by pressing situations to roll up their sleeves and do something. The fourth-century B.C. Taoist philosopher Chuang Tzu makes fun of them as perpetual busybodies, observing forms meticulously, rectifying names pedantically, preaching altruistic principles endlessly. No doubt the ordinary Confucian as a caricature of Confucius easily becomes ridiculous. But most people who have tried to practice the Confucian principles on the basis of their own reading of the Confucian texts, as most of the governors of the Chinese in the last two thousand years have done, are forcefully reminded of the sage's great practical common sense and are usefully instructed by his keen observation of human nature. To have united these realistic features with a continually inspiring sense of the nobility of human life is Confucius' lasting contribution to Chinese civilization. And to have done this so enduringly, while himself remaining just a man whose reasonable humanity could not be obscured, preventing all later misbegotten attempts to deify him, is a great achievement indeed. Every Chinese, educated or illiterate, growing up on the *Analects* as a text to be studied or as the common stuff of daily speech, has felt perhaps as if he lived with Confucius peering over his shoulder. But if so, the Chinese have lived with a benignly avuncular specter, one with whom a man could even talk lightly and share honest humor, not a fear-inspiring monster. To have remained a mere man while assuming so momentous a role in history is the rarest of human achievements.

Mencius

Mencius is the Latinized form of the name of Meng K'o. He lived from about 372 to 289 B.C. and was a native of the very small state called Tsou, lying adjacent to Confucius' native state of Lu, and similar to it in cultural traditions. He is the second great figure in the development of Confucian thought.

During the century between the death of Confucius and the birth of Mencius, no single figure had the stature to dominate the school of thought he had created. His disciples tended to emphasize distinct aspects of his teachings; narrower minds often failed to grasp the full scope of his thinking and became ever more absorbed in pursuing ever smaller aspects of it. Separate traditions associated with "genealogies" of master-student relationships developed. Some late Chou accounts refer to three or four distinct Confucian schools that acquired some identity of their own. One stressed filial piety and the spiritual and ethical concerns of the teachings. A second school became deeply involved in the study of ritual (*li*), and tended to regard ceremonies as formal religious observances to be more rigidly observed than Confucius seems to have intended, and as more directly regulative in their social implications. A third school stressed the practice of politics. And a fourth school became noted for its purely philosophical and even metaphysical specialization. These separate schools with their special characteristics need not be decried as degenerations of the founder's spirit. They also manifest the Confucian school's capacity for growth and accommodation to the new needs of a rapidly maturing civilization.

By the time Mencius appeared on the scene, he himself provides evidence of the degree to which certain Confucian innovations had become standard features of the society. Confucianism was a school of teachings, and its method of education really set it apart. The profession of the teacher was by Mencius' time well established; so also was the idea of "getting an education" as preparation for a career. Since the Confucian education meant above all access to and study of books, a great deal of the energy of the society went into copying and circulating texts, recording interpretations of them, and arguing about them. The "author" idea had appeared, although philosophical discourse was still primarily oral. Distinct positions in thought beyond the Confucian school had emerged, and debates between thinkers had become a standard activity both at courts, where such debates always had implications for government policy, and in the marketplace, where they were a form of entertainment.

This was the height of the Golden Age of Chinese philosophy; all the conditions of the time made for diversity and encouraged originality—an originality limited only by the crucial fact of the cultural monism of the ancient Chinese world. The ancient Mediterranean was a culturally pluralistic world of great diversity, albeit of high-level communication and dissemination of ideas. The Chinese, in contrast, knew no other high civilization until they became vaguely, distantly, and inaccurately aware of India through Buddhism half a millennium or more later, and not really directly until the West began to make a significant impact on Chinese minds in the nineteenth century.

But within the culturally single world of ancient China there existed, in those last preimperial centuries, certain conditions of diversity that were scarcely ever achieved again. There were many states, more or less on a par with each other, competing openly for the best brains and the most effective state policies. There was an increasing measure of social mobility breaking down the earlier conformity within fixed social classes. There was no sense of state orthodoxy, except in one or two exceptional states and for relatively short periods; competition among ideas and schools of thought was not limited. The wandering teacher-scholar-expert role that Confucius had played with such indifferent results had become a recognized public role of importance. Mencius exemplified it to the full. Great public interest in such figures and their ideas followed their appearances at the ducal courts of the time and encouraged response to their ideas. Finally, it was a period of disorder and dislocation creating serious problems in whose solution many people had an interest, and most people felt that such problems were challenges to their ingenuity, ethical sense, learning, or other human capacities. Hence the great burgeoning of thought.

Mencius was like Confucius in being considered the most learned man of his age. He was generally acknowledged by the Confucians of his time as their spokesman; he restored to the Confucian school a unity and cohesion it had lacked since the death of Confucius. But the changes that had occurred, especially the growth of the school itself, made Mencius' role quite unlike that of Confucius. He could travel about with all the pretensions and sense of self-importance appropriate to the successful spokesman of a great movement. And he did. There is more than just a suggestion that Mencius was a man who took himself rather seriously, was almost pompous in his bearing. His entourage resembled that of the great lords and kings.

Yet there is also a great sense of his expansive nature, his warmth of personality, and his vast spirit. It is easier to caricature him than any other great figure in Confucian history, but the apt caricature cannot deprive his personality of its undoubted force and value. His book, the *Mencius*, is of considerably greater bulk than *The Analects*. It probably was written by the man himself in the sense that he went over it as a text and improved it as a permanent record of his ideas. It has more linguistic unity than *The Analects*, but it still is more a record of perhaps idealized conversations than a collection of literary essays to be read—let alone to be read as formal philosophical arguments.

Mencius made his greatest contributions to Confucian thought in two widely separated areas. In each he took problems inherited from Confucius, problems which because of the incomplete stage of their development in the master's thought had become grounds of contention among later Confucians. In each he pressed for solutions that go distinctly beyond the record of Confucius' own thought, although they are made to seem quite logical extensions of Confucian viewpoints. The first is his contribution to the theory of human nature; the second lies in the area of political theory. Both reflect the typical concern with psychological issues, even though this may not be immediately apparent in the case of the second.

Confucius does not give a clear-cut answer to the question about the basic quality of human nature, probably because the question itself was not formulated so early. But his great emphasis on human psychology in relation to ethical problems made it inevitable that the problem of whether human nature was fundamentally good or bad would eventually arise. Confucius spoke constantly about *jen* (benevolence or goodness); making a sharp distinction between righteousness and profit, he said that a man of *jen* must strive for righteousness* and ignore issues of immediate profit or benefit. He never gave an adequate theoretical explanation of what it is in human nature that makes a person wish to be so altruistic. So many theories began to be discussed, for example, that individuals were good, or bad, or neutral, or both good and bad, or that some are good and others are bad. Mencius argued with proponents of the various theories, insisting that all people are clearly good by nature. Hsün Tzu in the next generation insisted on the opposite answer and, in their ways, both are equally Confucian. Eventually Confucianism developed some compromise solutions, but historically the Mencian solution to this philosophical problem ultimately became the more important and influential one among theorizers, even if Hsün Tzu's views long seemed more realistic to the doers.

Mencius said that all people are good at birth, but that they may be corrupted into developing bad practices and habits of mind by the environment about them unless they strive to preserve and develop their innate goodness. All people have their animal nature which—in distinctive Chinese fashion—is neither good nor bad in itself, but which is capable of making everyone do bad things to himself or herself and to others. Everyone is born with the incipient beginnings or the "buds" of benevolence or goodness (*jen*); righteousness (*yi*); respect or

---

* "Rightness, acting with a sense of justice"; the Chinese word lacks the sense of smug self-righteousness the English word may connote.

propriety (*li*); and the knowing capacity, especially the capacity to distinguish good from bad (*chih*). These moral capacities are innate, and each person must let them develop fully and express themselves in mature ethical behavior. They can be obscured, but not totally obliterated. His proof, typically a proof not theoretically sound, but simply an apt and compelling observation of human psychology, is that the basest scoundrel, on seeing a child teetering at the edge of a well in peril of falling in and drowning, would instinctively be moved to commiseration and would try to rescue the child without hesitating even a moment to calculate issues of advantage. Lest this "proof" of an important point about human nature seem evidence of Mencius' simple-mindedness, it should be noted that he offers very sophisticated discussions of the differences between human and animal nature, of the way a person's material and sexual needs may override one's humane judgment, and of the effects of environment on human nature. He had a subtle appreciation for all the complexities of human life, and yet he remained optimistic about it.

People, having the four inherent moral tendencies, should then cultivate them to the limit, and the limit in any case is ultimate perfection. All human nature is ultimately perfectible; its innate qualities imply an egalitarian view of human nature itself and an extreme optimism about humanity and society. This optimism contributed to the Confucian theory of education, both furthering its already egalitarian spirit and stressing its social significance. The way to improve society clearly was to bring to its service the best among its latent human resources. Mencius' view that all people are potential sages enhanced the perception of fundamental dignity; this helped to maintain the humanistic import of Confucianism.

Mencius' political theory went even further. According to Confucius and the Confucian school generally, the state exists because it ought to exist, because it is the logical culmination of natural human relationships. It has ethical significance because people are meant to associate with other people in ways that tend to bring out the best in everyone; such an association of humanity in society naturally implies the existence of the state. But the kind of state is not specified. The options were not many. Nothing but the monarchical family-state had ever existed in the ken of any Chinese, and the assumption in the minds of all Chinese was that some form of monarchy centralizing ultimate political authority would have to exist. Within that definition of the form of the state, a range of possibilities existed.

Mencius lived in times even more troubled than those of Confucius, the date of whose death conventionally begins an era known as the Period of the Warring States. Two kinds of government, or two poles in a spectrum of types, existed in Mencius' eyes. At one end, existing mainly in the idealized historical memory of the Chinese, was "kingly" government. At the other end was government by naked force, exercised in the name of a king by a military overlord or *pa*. The progressive militarization of society in this period produced ever more of the latter and with it ever more wars and violence. Mencius was extremely sensitive to the people's sufferings because of violence and disorder, so he railed constantly against the evils of government by force. Utilizing the doctrine of the rectification of names, he declared that when a ruler fails to be a kingly ruler, he is no longer a king and the people have the right to resist him, to rebel against him, and if necessary even to kill him in the course of rebellion, for by that doctrine "tyrannicide is not regicide."

This position seems to make Mencius a political radical. In fact his position is philosophically radical but politically conservative, in some ways rather more so than that of Confucius. Philosophically, however, Mencius proposed a doctrine that is, while not explicitly anthropocentric, nonetheless quite radically humanistic: By the logical extension of the right to rebellion, he declared that the people are the most important element in a state and the ruler the least important. He went still further and said that the Mandate of Heaven that gave the ruler his position was tantamount to the expression of the people's satisfaction. By saying "Heaven hears as the people hear; Heaven sees as the people see," Mencius not only made the people the ultimate standard for judging government, but made man the standard for Heaven itself. "Heaven" to Mencius meant Nature, or the ethical cosmic order *in toto*. That does not, to be sure, say that the universe is to be viewed *only* in terms of human experience, but it takes the well-being of human society as the measure of Nature's proper functioning. It is an uncompromising statement of humanism. At the same time, in political-science terminology, "Mencius believed that the ultimate sovereignty lay with the people."* Yet he did not propose institutional changes that would go beyond his concern "for the people" to achieve

---

* K. C. Hsiao. *A History of Chinese Political Thought*. English edition. Princeton, N.J.: Princeton University Press, 1979, p. 158.

government "by the people." "Heaven's agent," meaning a new dynastic founder, would restore benevolent government for the good of the people in due time.

Mencius left a set of political propositions that on the surface seem to embody a number of unresolved contradictions. Some of them are as follows:

1a. Mencius said every man can be a Yao or a Shun (perfect sage).
  b. Mencius urged that hereditary official emolument should be restored.
2a. Mencius stressed the appropriateness of ancient models, although not exclusively those of the Chou dynasty.
  b. Mencius spoke with anticipation of a new order to be founded by a new king.
3a. Mencius courageously told kings to their faces that the common people were more important than themselves.
  b. Mencius justified the privileges and prerogatives of the ruling aristocracy (yet told kings that their relatives should be sacked if they could not serve the people's needs).
4a. Mencius urged the loyalty of scholars to rulers.
  b. Mencius approved of rebellion, even of tyrannicide.

These sets of apparently contradictory statements can be taken as parts of a whole view of society and government in which the inner consistency stems from Mencius' basic concepts: that jen is the way of government, that to nourish the people is the prime task of government, and that the commiserating human mind-heart (jen-hsin) is the instrument of the government. The doctrine of "the rectification of names" readily solves the apparent problem in number 4, for example.

To Confucius the proper models of government lay quite literally in the Institutes of Chou. To Mencius they lay in ideals he himself formulated out of a broader view of the mythologized past, and they thus transcended the limitations of Chou models. Confucius would have been scandalized! But, it will be remembered, neither man had more than minimal involvement in the actual tasks of government. Hsün Tzu, on the other hand, whose active years followed closely after Mencius' death, knew the day-to-day work of government from long years of service. To Hsün Tzu, the models of government lay in the concrete and rationally apprehended normative institutions of the entire Great Tradition, especially in its li or ritual ordinances. These norms of government were validated not by reference to any particular period of history in the literal sense, but by their pragmatic effectiveness. He was therefore still more ready than Mencius to see the end of the long-defunct Chou order and its replacement by something that would work better. Confucius, Mencius, and Hsün Tzu reflect three differing personalities and temperaments and also widely differing and progressively worsening disorders and political breakdown. At the same time, we must assume that the cultural level of the Chinese continuously advanced and matured, forcing political thinkers to address themselves to ever higher levels of political expectations.

Mencius is also important in the development of the Confucian school for pushing its thought in the direction of philosophical mysticism. Mysticism implies idealistic monism; that is, philosophical mysticism is a conception of reality as an extension of the mind and of the gnostic desirability of achieving some kind of awareness of the oneness of the knower and the known. Although Mencius is true to the Confucian orientation in being concerned primarily with the good of society here and now and with the practical and ethical concerns of life, these are not contradictory to philosophical (as opposed to primarily religious) mysticism. Mencius established a Confucian ground for the subsequent development of thought in this direction, although for his time and some centuries thereafter Taoist thought was much more active in those pursuits.

Mencius said that when man develops his mind, he knows his nature, and when he knows his own nature, he knows Heaven—by which he meant Nature or the cosmic order. He also said that there is a great ch'i (literally, "breath"; probably to Mencius some kind of vital spirit that pervades humanity and the universe). Everyone can develop this within oneself. "When I nourish this great breath within me," Mencius wrote, "all things are then complete within me." He acknowledged that this was hard to understand and did not offer a full discussion of it. Yet it is central to his thought. It shows the great scope of the Confucian intellectual world and the range of problems it could legitimately claim as its own without abandoning its essential character.

The polarization of the Confucian intellectual sphere was accomplished very soon thereafter by Hsün Tzu, who disagreed with Mencius on many things and whose influence on Confucian thought was much the greater during the first thousand years of the imperial period. We tend to forget this, because Neo-Confucianism has meant a great comeback for Mencius, who—nominally at least—dominated China's view of Confucian truth during the second thousand years of the imperial period, a millennium that has provided the lenses through which the Chinese of today as well as we ourselves largely see the Chinese past.

Hsün Tzu

Hsün Ch'ing, who also had the given name of K'uang, never was important enough in the centuries of Western knowledge of China for his name to have been Latinized, otherwise we might be calling him Hsüncius. He lived from about 298 to 238 B.C. and was the last great mind to appear in the Confucian school before the imperial period. His impact on Confucian thought was initially very great, and throughout history Hsün Tzu's orderly way of thinking has continued to appeal to many. Like Confucius and Mencius, he was a native of North China, and like them he was acknowledged to be the most learned man of his time. But unlike them, he spent the greatest part of his active life as a regional administrator in the local government of central China. He was therefore the first great Confucian philosopher to establish what was to become a pattern for the imperial period—the philosopher who devotes much of his life to the practical affairs of government.

Also Hsün Tzu was the first Confucian who wrote his works as philosophical arguments, as essays for other people to read. Thus we get from him fuller statements of problems and much fuller development of argumentation than we find in either Confucius or Mencius. He is much more satisfying and perhaps more convincing to read as a philosopher. Beyond that, however, he also had by far the most orderly mind in early Chinese thought. A no-nonsense toughness of mind and precision of statement comes through to the modern reader with force and clarity.

Hsün Tzu had the bad fortune to teach two bright young men who later left his school and repudiated Confucian teaching to take up the Legalist doctrines then competing actively with Confucianism as a theory of government. Since these two, the philosopher Han Fei Tzu and the statesman Li Ssu, made incalculable contributions to the success of the Legalist state of Ch'in in unifying the world through military conquest and creating the Chinese empire, for which achievement Ch'in was forever publicly hated (and secretly admired?), and since the teacher-student relationship created responsibilities that cut both ways, Hsün Tzu has sometimes been looked upon as a traitor to Confucianism, a kind of proto-Legalist.

He was neither. He was completely faithful to the concept of an ethical universe and of government for the good of the governed. But he was at the polar extreme from Mencius within the Confucian world of ideas, and to some that has made his rigorously pursued and hard-headed ideas seem congenial to the spirit of Legalism. There is·at least no doubt that he believed in the necessity for a strong and highly centralized government in which the position of the ruler would be elevated to heights unknown to that time. Nonetheless he totally disagreed with the Legalists' notion that the people and the state existed to give power to the ruler. In this he agreed with Mencius (although he argued it differently) that the ruler existed solely to serve the well-being of the people, as a majestic public servant, and when he failed in that overriding duty, he should be deposed.

It is revealing to compare Hsün Tzu and Mencius in their attitudes toward some basic issues of the times. On the quality and tone of government, Hsün Tzu expected it to be authoritarian, and Mencius assumed it should be liberal and permissive. On ethics Hsün Tzu proposed highly normative, objectively imposed ethical standards to be inculcated by intensive education and, backed up by social convention, enforced by the power of the state; Mencius insisted on the subjective nature of the innate ethical sense, the individual's free expression of it. Hsün Tzu regarded civilization as humanity's triumph over itself, and Mencius looked upon it as humanity's cumulative expression of itself. Hsün Tzu saw humanity apart from nature and valued its ability to create the artificial; Mencius hinted at the awareness of a "mystical oneness" of humankind and nature. Yet throughout these sets of polar views there runs a Confucian thread. Both believe in government, both accept the rightness of absolute ethical values, both value civilization, and both regard humanity as more important than the rest of nature. Legalists could not agree with either man on the second of these points nor in their manner of dealing with the others. And Taoists would have to disagree fundamentally on all four points.

It is sometimes said that Mencius and Hsün Tzu represent the "left" and "right" wings of the Confucian tradition. This is suggestive, but on examination seems not to be entirely useful. If Mencius is leftist for stressing individual freedom over social control, Hsün Tzu is more liberal in repudiating any dogmatic foundations of ethics. Mencius' subjective idealism in ethical and intellectual matters comes dangerously close to producing supermoral values that deny reason and lead easily to arbitrary authoritarianism—a trap from which the left in our time has had great difficulty remaining free. A stultifying moral zeal was one of the diseases of Neo-Confucianism, and it is also interesting to note that Neo-Confucianism, which honored Mencius above Hsün Tzu as the prime follower of Confucius, became the orthodoxy of the Chinese state in the period of its most extreme authoritarianism. In all fairness, however, we can no more blame Mencius for that than we can blame Hsün Tzu for the Legalist triumph, or Plato for Hitler.

The ideas of Hsün Tzu and Mencius are most frequently contrasted at the point of their views of human nature. Hsün Tzu said that our basic nature is slothful, lustful, avaricious, and animal, and that instead of freely expressing that nature, we must curb and refine it, to replace that which is of nature with that which society has made, that is, with culture. This was, however, urged for the good of society, not for any salvation of anyone's soul. The West's theologically buttressed predilections are to read into Hsün Tzu some intimation of original sin or find some confirmation of its own view that human nature rests in a God-created cosmos. The disagreement between Mencius and Hsün Tzu has thus tended to assume proportions it never had in the traditional Chinese view. For although the two squarely disagreed on the definition of the basic human nature and although Hsün Tzu expressed his disagreement with his predecessor in terms that revealed his general contempt for Mencius' intellectual capacities, of far greater importance in the history of Confucian thought has been their complete agreement on the perfectibility of humankind.

Hsün Tzu had neither a low nor a pessimistic view of humanity. Human culture, in his view, is the noblest thing in the world and is proof of our capacity to triumph over our nature. He saw people as born with incipient wisdom—even animal-man knows a good thing when he sees it—and this wisdom led the wisest of people to invent the institutions and conventions of civilization, as it has led lesser people to accept and preserve these. This ultimate agreement on our perfectibility through education led both philosophers to stress the importance of personal cultivation and of formal training in historical and classical studies.

Hsün Tzu's philosophy has been called a philosophy of culture. The pursuit and refinement of culture, he believed, is a person's basic vocation. And the core of that culture is *li*, the ritual ordinances governing behavior. *Li*, in the thought of Hsün Tzu, became a comprehensive idea, involving ceremonies, rituals, the rules of social conduct, the norms of political behavior, and the private standards by which one governs one's own emotions and actions. In society at large, the *li* sets reasonable limits to the satisfaction of desires. The ceremonies and rituals of *li* refine and purify the emotions and senses of the persons participating in them or observing others perform them.

A person, said Hsün Tzu, is not a person by reason of upright posture, ability to speak, or any other crude distinguishing features. A person is a person by reason of the ability to make distinctions and to form groups for cooperative action. Above all, the mind's capacity to refine and classify data interested Hsün Tzu, and his writings give great attention to precision in the meanings of terms and in establishing categories of terms and relationships. His was a systematizing mind. He felt that our ability to observe social differences natural and normal to human society preserved the only workable social system. The correct observance of the differing roles of ruler and minister preserved politics, just as the correct separation of the roles of male and female, father and son, preserved the functioning family and the orderly society. The *li* were institutionalizations of these distinctions, and at the same time transcendent expressions of their spiritual value. Human intelligence leads us to submit to them.

Submitting to imposed norms, if one has the intelligence to do so, and finding value in so doing is the essence of Hsün Tzu's social and political thought. His was a mind of great range. Like the stereotype of the learned Confucian of later ages, Hsün Tzu had a deep appreciation for literature and was a skilled musician. As a great scholar of his cultural tradition, he had original views about some features of it. He also had a sharp mind for intellectual debate; his arguments with Taoists and Mohists and others will be discussed in that connection in Chapter 5.

Finally it is worth noting that Hsün Tzu tried to take the mystery out of society's relations with the natural world. In strongly rationalistic tones he argued that heaven, or nature, went its own way according to its principles; it did not possess a will to intervene in human affairs. Mencius had stressed heaven's will as a factor in human life. Hsün Tzu wrote at length and cogently about the distinction between heaven and people, saying that people should not seek to interpret natural phenomena, even unusual prodigies and calamities, as signs to humans or as indications of cosmic intent to guide the ruler and the state. He did not have great success in convincing ordinary people, and even among Confucian thinkers the notion of heavenly portents may have seemed a useful instrument for curbing despots. In later ages the rationalistic strain frequently had its effective spokesmen and was always present in some measure, but it did not often dominate the world of thought.

Looking back we can conclude that Confucius, Mencius, and Hsün Tzu, the three great figures in early Confucianism, display well the range of ideas and personality types possible within the Confucian school. Looking ahead we can anticipate the vitality as well as the tensions that were to be generated within it, as the Confucian intellectual world continued to enlarge its horizons. As it grew, it remained the principal guide to Chinese civilization thereafter, yet retained the essential qualities that these three figures had imparted to it.

Chapter Four
Early Taoism

Throughout most of Chinese history, Confucianism has been the proper, openly espoused, official, and, in the limited sense that the word has application in China, the orthodox system of thought. It has been the great way of the whole civilization, the mainstream of intellectual life, the dominant mode of social and political existence. Yet in no period of Chinese history has Confucianism encompassed all there was to China's intellectual and cultural life. Confucian rationalism, suspended judgment, ethical sense, and sober practicality all had their opposed counterparts in a complementary minor mode of the civilization. And characteristically it was this minor mode, Taoism, that sustained those imaginative and unbridled minds that have appeared as frequently among the Chinese as among any people.

From this other current in the intellectual life sprang much of the more allusive and fanciful poetry, the stranger and more expressionistic currents in painting, the introspective and more intuitive reaches in philosophy. In the earlier periods of history, from Confucius well into the imperial era, this other current can be clearly labeled Taoist; after the third or fourth centuries A.D. the labels become less clear, though the currents continue.

That is not to say that Confucians were dull fellows. There is in

Confucianism a great vitality, a keen enjoyment of life and a sense of humor, a profound appreciation of music and literature and, after their fashion, a steady encouragement of art and poetry. But in Confucianism there is little speculation about the unreal or the impractical and little interest in that which seems too far removed from normal daily life, too far outside the realm of common sense. In its early philosophy the questions about ultimate reality are not even raised. The material world is accepted and unquestioned, and the real issues before people throughout Confucian history are the social-ethical issues of this present real world. Not surprisingly there were people who were not interested in a Confucian endorsement.

Relationship to Confucianism

Taoism presents another side of the Chinese mind. Throughout most of Chinese history Taoism has been a fascinating realm of speculative thought for many people. It has steadfastly—and usually wittily—repudiated the ethics of Confucianism and all other "artificial devices" of civilization. It has mocked ritual and propriety and decried the group conventions. It has urged egocentric individualism as persuasively for some as Confucianism has stressed the development of the individual through proper performance of his role within the social system for the rest. Although accepted with equanimity by most, it has seemed pernicious and positively dangerous to some few, among whom have been certain thoughtful Confucians and more shallow-minded conformists little moved by ideas as such. Again, in viewing these competing systems of ideas, we must avoid easy analogies to our own history. The Chinese throughout their history were deprived of the dubious blessings of any "jealous god" notions that might encourage an acceptance of exclusive truth in philosophy and religion. And so, to the vast majority, Confucianism and Taoism have been complementary, not mutually exclusive, views of life. Confucian optimistic rationalism in its social-mindedness and Taoist pessimistic mysticism in its extreme individualism, mutually contradictory as they can be on the levels of both theory and practice, nonetheless have related to each other like the opposite sides of one coin or the two poles of one axis. Their union as parts of one coin or one axis, as aspects of one Chinese civilization, has been more important than hostility between them. We should therefore avoid what is in fact our cultural parochialism when we read into the Confucian-Taoist, or eventually the Confucian-Taoist-Buddhist relationship, the kind of opposition that we consider natural to competing ideas or hostile religions—natural to us only because it has been a familiar component of our tradition.

The image of Taoism in Chinese history is complicated by the fact that *Tao* has a considerable range of possible meanings, but even more because Taoism can refer to many things, from the writings of philosophers to the cultic practices of popular religion. There came to be two levels of Taoism's existence, merging somewhat at the middle while differing so much at the extremes that they were incompatible. Taoism was subject to no unifying authority imposed upon it by its own loose organizational forms or from above. Thus philosophical Taoism came to be as different from religious Taoism—despite common veneration of Lao Tzu and other real or mythologized figures, common jargon, and common central texts—as it was from Confucianism. Despite the tensions between those extremes, they usually coexisted in the general atmosphere of tolerance for all varieties of life and thought so long as social order was not threatened. The philosophical Taoist whose highest ideal was the acceptance of Nature and the Taoist magician (a gross caricature of the philosopher) whose alchemy was aimed at the conquest of nature nonetheless continued to exist side by side and to be somewhat unsure where the boundary between their Taoisms should lie.

If most thinking Confucians have been critical of Taoism, it has been to dissociate themselves from that form of Taoism that was no longer philosophically interesting either to them or to philosophical-minded Taoists. Vulgarized Taoism also became understandably a bit scandalous in the eyes of propriety-minded upper-class types, though that did not keep them from enjoying the magic and fortunetelling and other colorful aspects—"just for amusement," of course. On all levels Taoism had great appeal for the romantics and the credulous, the frustrated and the unstable, and it was therefore susceptible to kinds of flimsy fancy that Confucianism was spared. At the same time it was the principal element in the daily religious life of most of the common people, even though it later shared that ground with popular Buddhism. But that is to anticipate its later social history.

In intellectual content philosophical Taoism is fundamentally at variance with Confucianism. Most serious Confucian and Taoist thinkers of the Golden Age in preimperial China were quite aware of this, and they have striven to clarify the distinctions so as to make the larger truth of the one or the other stand out. We, looking at them from the outside, are struck by the Chineseness of both. Both display the same predilection for concepts by intuition rather than by postulation, for suggestive rather than explicit language, for similitude rather than syllogism. Both partake of the same worldliness, for although it did not value humankind's social world of civilization as the Confucians did, Taoism too is devoted to the problems of living in this world here and now. Taoism is also concerned with observations of nature, though it pursues cosmological reflections upon nature more avidly than early Confucianism ever did. Both accept the concept of the harmonious and organic interplay of the complementary, quasi-cosmological forces (yin-yang) as an explanation of observed change in the world. But, unlike Confucianism, Taoism focuses upon and idealizes nature.

The principle "reversal is the movement of Tao" lies at the very heart of Taoism and is illustrated for the Taoist mind by reference to all kinds of phenomena observed in nature. In contrast the Confucian tends to verify his central tenets by observations of human psychology. To identify the issue on which the two philosophies split most clearly, Confucianism believes that a person should live in harmony with nature and other people, but that a person is the measure of Confucian values. Hence we call it a *humanism*—as unequivocal as the world has known. In contrast Taoism sees a person as ideally living in harmony with nature and if necessary isolated from other people. Nature, not people, is the touchstone of Taoist values. Hence we could call it a *naturalism*—and certainly an extreme one. The terms are somewhat confused for us by the fact that in the West humanism promoted a romantic and idealistic view of nature, and in that pattern associated the two; in China, on the contrary, humanism and naturalism (in that special sense of idealizing nature) mark the poles of philosophy.

In intellectual history, however, ideas are defined by the issues in response to which they develop. Humanism in the West developed in response to (or against) religious authoritarianism, and pagan nature was readily associable with its humanism for historical and cultural reasons. In China Taoist idealization of nature was part of a pessimism about humanity's capacity to keep order and safety in society; it sought nature as a refuge from humanity. There is nothing intrinsically more reasonable in the one set of associations than in the other.

Taoism therefore came to regard social man as a misguided being. It scorned government, feared progress and civilization, and was wary of all kinds of technical skills. It came to see all standards, definitions, distinctions, and classifications (in which Confucianism placed such value) as degenerating devices destructive to the healthy state of pristine nature. It emerged in an age of social disorder—as did Confucianism—and its obsession came to be the preservation of life. It withdrew to nature because it found human society too hazardous. That negative attitude alone is not a philosophy, but from such a basic position a philosophy could develop. It did, and eventually it became a subtle and sophisticated structure of ideas.

Who Was Lao Tzu?

Ssu-ma Ch'ien, the great historian of the late second and early first centuries B.C., in writing his Shih Chi (Records of the Grand Historian) faced a real problem in Lao Tzu, the reputed founder of Taoism. Here was a figure so important to the Chinese historical consciousness that he could not be ignored. Yet Ssu-ma Ch'ien, even with the historical archives available to him and after his father's and his own decades of judging and ordering the historical materials, could not decide which of the traditions associated with him, covering a span of several centuries in their time references, could really apply to the man credited with the authorship of the Tao Te Ching. Was it that Lao Tzu whom Confucius visited, the venerable keeper of the archives of Chou whom Confucius consulted about the ancient records of rituals? Or was it any of several semihistorical personages of the next two or three centuries? Ssu-ma Ch'ien was a careful historian; unable to solve this riddle, he presents various versions for us to judge for ourselves. The riddle has been with us ever since.

In the early years of the twentieth century, scholars in China and in the West, feeling the responsibility to be yet more skeptical (ergo more "scientific") than their predecessors, were often overly suspicious of early Chinese traditions. Much was rejected for reasons that were ill-considered and shallow. More recently the material evidence provided by archeology frequently has validated earlier traditions, and there has been a retreat from the high tide of skepticism and iconoclasm. There is still no full agreement about who wrote the Tao Te

Ching or when it was first put into the form in which we know it, but there seems to be no reason to doubt that Confucius met an elderly keeper of archives in the Royal Chou domain whose name was Li Erh, but who may also have been called Lao Tzu, meaning "the old philosopher." And there are strong although by no means universally accepted reasons for believing that the *Tao Te Ching*—or at least its central ideas—could have come into being at that time, whether or not the old archivist or some near contemporary was its author.* In fact there are good reasons for considering the fundamental philosophy of that book to have taken form more or less at the time of Confucius. We shall adopt that view, though acknowledging the many foggy aspects of early Taoism's history.

This does not mean that we need to be more than amused, as generations of Chinese have been amused, by the fanciful myths about Lao Tzu. One of these tells that Lao Tzu's mother was pregnant with him for decades, so that when he finally emerged from her womb, he had a long white beard and walked with a cane—hence his name Lao Tzu, which also can mean "the old child." Another tells that after many years of service as keeper of the archives, the venerable philosopher left China to "go west" into Central Asia. As he passed through the Great Wall or some western gateway of a wall that existed then, the gatekeeper got him to write down his teachings. These were put down in five thousand characters, the text of the *Tao Te Ching*. Then he walked on to the west and disappeared. Later Taoists, trying to elevate their doctrine above Buddhism, claimed with mock seriousness that he went on to India, where he taught the Buddha who, of course, learned only imperfectly. These stories reveal something of the flavor of Chinese civilization and of Taoism's role in the folk culture particularly. We need hardly expect them also to reveal the precise, mundane history of the founder of Taoism.

It is more reasonable to assume that Taoism had no single founder. We have presented Confucianism as a school of thought drawing on well-established elements of the Great Tradition of Chinese civilization, but taking distinctive new form and quality because of its founder's personal achievements. In that sense Confucianism has a

---

* See the discussion of the dating of the *Tao Te Ching* in W.T. Chan, *The Way of Lao Tzu.*

founding figure, even though the Chinese have not called the movement by his name as we do in English. In English we do not label the Taoist movement by any personal name, but we do simplify it in another way by calling all aspects of it Taoist. In Chinese it has historically had a number of designations more appropriate to its periods and parts, though undoubtedly all the aspects and achievements that might be ascribed to a founding figure of everything we call Taoism have gathered around the somewhat mythologized person Lao Tzu and are associated with the *Tao Te Ching* as his statement of truths.

We might posit the hypothesis that after Confucius had taken a stand in the world of thought and had begun to earn some awareness of his system of ideas, the intellectual currents at the other end of the magnetic field also polarized. It may well be that the active persons in this development attributed their ideas to some prestigious figure like the venerable archivist of Chou who had to be acknowledged senior to Confucius even by the philosopher himself, since Confucius had gone to consult with and learn from him. It may also be true that the historical Lao Tzu was in his own right a leading personality within the field of thought that eventually became identified with the name of Taoism and that the ideas of the book may indeed even have taken their decisive literary form from some such person. The riddle must remain a riddle, but the early emergence of Taoist thought need not be doubted. Many kinds of internal evidence support such a conclusion.

On the other hand, the early emergence of such a system of thought and its formulation in a book is not in itself proof of the existence from the beginning of the *Tao Te Ching* as we now know it. Some scholars find the text of the book so subtle in its thought and expression that they feel it must be later than the *Chuang Tzu*, the other great work of early Taoism whose author, Chuang Chou, died about 286 B.C. Others see the content of its thought directly derivative from the *Chuang Tzu* and thus date the *Tao Te Ching* to the mid-third century B.C. or even later. All doubts about the dating of the book as we now know it must remain unresolved questions until the Chinese recover the *ur*-text or other very early evidence in some archeological find. In the meantime the view tentatively adopted here is that someone, perhaps called Lao Tzu, wrote a *Tao Te Ching* about the time of Confucius when the basic ideas of Taoist thought were taking shape.

That book was transmitted and in the process probably refined, perhaps to incorporate some later and more sophisticated ideas. But the thought system and the mode of expression are those of an earlier and simpler, not a post-Chuangtzian, phase of Taoist thought. Much of the current opinion, to be sure, varies from this view in greater or lesser extent, yet the view that the book is an early attempt to formulate elusive yet basically simple ideas remains very persuasive.

The Tao Te Ching is a book in poetic form composed in highly allusive language. In part this is a conscious device to convey the inexpressible, for Taoism faced the classic difficulty of all mysticisms in trying to talk about what it believed could not be contained in words. But the linguistic vagueness of the book also stems from another difficulty, that of trying to devise a jargon for philosophical discourse. Such a word as tao, literally "a roadway," had already acquired extended meanings of "a way" or "the way." In both Confucian and Taoist usage it was being further extended at this time to mean "the Way," or "the great Way of the kings of antiquity" (in Confucianism) and "the great Way of nature and the cosmos" (in Taoism). Taoism takes its name from this key concept of the system; simultaneously the word in its distinct Confucian sense of "the ethical Way" also became fixed, and remained current in later usage to modern times. If the Confucian usage had been fixed first, it seems difficult to imagine that the Taoists would have insisted on appropriating that term for so central a purpose. It is more likely that these two specialized extensions of its meaning were being worked out at the same time and became fixed simultaneously as equally acceptable specialized definitions, neither having priority over the other. For the Confucians never argue that tao does not mean what the Taoists say it means, nor do Taoists ever argue that tao cannot mean what the competing Confucians have long said it meant. Without developing a full battery of such arguments, it can be seen that there are reasons for regarding the period of the Tao Te Ching as roughly the period of Confucius. It was the period in which the initial philosophical responses to the difficulties of life in late Chou China were beginning to be articulated; both traditions shared many linguistic as well as conceptualizing difficulties in their parallel tasks of articulating ideas.

It is illuminating to observe what widely varying philosophical reactions to the same set of historical conditions the late Chou age could produce. Confucianism drew the extroverted, activist types to its positive doctrines for improving the world. Taoism became at first the somewhat humorously jaundiced commentary on activism and do-goodism, then found in the passive stance a more profound philosophy than mere defeatism. For all the difficulties of enunciating such a philosophy, Taoism achieves a beguiling expression in the *Tao Te Ching*.

The Content of the *Tao Te Ching*

One of the world's most frequently translated books, the *Tao Te Ching* exists in dozens of English versions which vary not just widely but wildly in their interpretations of its short text. In the final form in which the book has existed now for over fifteen hundred years, a rearrangement probably made in the third century A.D., it consists of eighty-one short chapters. Each is a poem-like statement of from a few dozen to a hundred characters in length. The whole is divided into two parts, for which the two characters of the title provide subtitles. That is, the first part (the book is variously divided) is given the name of the Book of *Tao* and the second, the Book of *Te*. *Ching* means canonical work or revered book. We have discussed the basic meanings of *tao*. *Te* is also a rather elusive concept, translated sometimes as "power" (Waley), meaning in later Chinese "virtue" or "the virtue of a thing," that is, its own character. The word is related to the word meaning "to obtain," and as used in the *Tao Te Ching* it appears to carry some of the meaning of "that which obtains," or the effects of that which obtains, the results. Perhaps then *tao* is the transcendent principle and *te* is its varied manifestation in concrete situations. When we seek out all the uses of these two words in the book, we find the following kinds of explanations and equations given there:

Tao:
the mother force (original force) of the cosmos
something without form or sound or substance
the "one"
the limitlessly vast, great; "to force a name on it we may say it is *jung*" ("capacious")
everlasting and unchanging ("the valley spirit does not die")
not contingent on anything, independent of everything

ceaselessly involved in circulatory motion
inexhaustible in use
functions as the natural process of nature
does nothing, yet accomplishes everything
unnamable and incapable of being spoken about

Te:
the great virtue or power that follows from tao
that which fosters or nurtures all things
that which guides things back to their original state
the character of the profoundly wise man
the fundamental character of everything that exists

From the preceding it appears that tao is the sum total of all te of all things. The te is the aspect of tao that can be known. Yet it is not the whole, but is merely as much as can be apprehended through knowledge of separate things. In fact, however, the tao is indivisible; hence, when known, it is wholly known. It has no parts. This is a paradox of tao and te. One line in the Chuang Tzu says: "That which pervades Heaven and Earth is tao; that which functions in harmony with Heaven and Earth is te; that which acts through all being is justice" (that is, "that which ought to be" in a naturalistic but not an ethical sense). Hence te is included within the concept of tao, but tao is merely implied by the concept of te.

The Tao Te Ching repeatedly speaks of the relation of tao to nature and the things in the world, humans included. It describes the process of production and dissolution of material things, or of the concentration and dispersion of matter. In certain places it says that tao produced the one, that the one produced the two, that the two produced the three, and that the three produced all things. This seems to make the tao the ultimate. But elsewhere it states that the ways of tao are conditioned by the "self-so" or nature. This seems to say that tao is not the ultimate, but that the "self-so" or spontaneous, ungenerated (or self-generated) nature is the ultimate.

Actually it is immaterial in which order these elements of the cosmogonic process are named, for all stages of the process are always simultaneously present; they are not intended to describe a process in time, a departure from a beginning point in history. The purpose is to convey merely the fact of flux, the unending, infinitely manifold process in the forms of things, over and beyond which (or underlying which, if that metaphor seems to imply more certain foundations) is the unchanging oneness, the unconditioned and unlimited *tao*.

To understand the *tao* is the great goal of the philosophical Taoist. If he cannot truly understand it, he can acquire confidence that it exists and observe its manifestations in nature. But if he can grasp its real nature, he will gain a mental clarity that will dissolve all other intellectual problems. Since the *tao* is one and indivisible, knowledge of it cannot be gained piecemeal, bit by bit. It is not a science; it cannot be the object of a cumulative learning process. The *Tao Te Ching* devises many metaphors to indicate this and to direct the knowing, seeking act inward. Ultimately the *tao* will be known, if at all, as an experience of oneness in which the knower becomes the *tao*, not through a transformation, but merely by gaining the awareness that all existence is one with his own mind.

This sudden illumination is common to all mysticisms, but Taoist mysticism displays some unusual cultural features. The Taoist is concerned with the intellectual or spiritual consequences of the experience, not (as in religious mysticisms) with enjoying the state of union as a divine experience to be sought for its own sake. Moreover Taoism is unusual in that it describes the *tao* and the state of union with it in negative terms, diminishing their sensory quality to nothingness. The *tao* is described as colorless, tasteless, pale and dim, thin and vague, lacking positive qualities of heightened sensory perception. Contrast this with the perception of ecstasy, the sweetness and ineffable fragrance, the blinding flash of light, the sexual analogies of almost all other mysticisms in describing the experience of union with the infinite, ineffable one.

What good to us then is the *tao*? None. Here we see most clearly the difference between philosophical and religious mysticism. The *tao* is useful, indeed essential to be sure, but it is that whether or not we want it to be so. We cannot invoke it. It will not help us in any specific sense. It is wholly impersonal. We cannot approach it in prayer or ask it to intercede for us. It has no attachment to the beings whose existence it assures. The *Tao Te Ching* says the *tao* is "unkind"; that is, it is not affected by human standards of morality and benevolence, nor indeed by anything. This contradicts as profoundly as possible the Confucian view of an "ethical cosmos," yet many Confucians were deeply influenced by the Taoist view, which they called "that vast conception." It is assuredly a vast idea, and it enlarged the philosophical world of ancient China.

If the tao is of no direct good to us, still understanding the nature of the universe is useful. The book has a common-sense level of meaning which offers advice on how to get along in the world. The message is, in Lin Yutang's apt phrase, a "philosophy of camouflage." It warns against striving and teaches the wisdom of lying low, of appearing foolish, of giving way and not contending for place or advantage. It teaches the relativity of truth and of all the standards of designing human minds. Above all it stresses the importance of simplicity in life style and in thought for the sake of harmony with the world about one, and the limited but practical freedom that brings.

The book also indicates that there is another level of usefulness in getting the message. There is the possibility of becoming an enlightened person: One who has known the tao in experience is thereafter transformed so that he or she seems powerfully different from ordinary persons. The Taoists succeeded in conveying to the masses of the people who had no expectation of ever having a mystical experience of their own that such in truth was possible and that a kind of super-sage who understood everything, but who did nothing, was the result. It had the consequence of making this conception very real in the world of Chinese culture. Because the enlightened person achieved absolute personal freedom from conventions, from attachment, and from all social entanglements, the value of seeking such freedom was kept alive and made meaningful for the whole society. The experiencing of this freedom was not a limited freedom *from* something, but was itself the way to the mystical apprehension of truth, the experiencing of ultimate reality.

The Tao Te Ching also could be read in more mundane ways. Taken literally the concept of te as the efficacious aspect of the tao, that is, its power, might be seen as a force for accomplishing specific immediate ends, almost a kind of magic, and hence something that people should strive to use for all kinds of calculated advantages. Where the philosopher wrote allusively about te as an aspect of cosmic function quite beyond human control, he wrote in metaphors intended to suggest vast ideas that lay beyond his words. A less well-attuned reader might read it as straightforward advice about making use of nature and people for less noble goals. So doing turns philosophy into manipulative tactics; it turns reflective, speculative pursuit of truth into political advice. The *Tao Te Ching* was quite susceptible to such uses.

An early tradition of using the *Tao Te Ching* as a practical handbook for winning at the world's political games has come to light through an immensely important archeological discovery of 1972 at Ma-wang-tui, a site near the provincial capital of Hunan Province. Here a complex of graves of members of an important family who died between 186 and 166 B.C. turned up phenomenally well-preserved corpses, funereal objects in profusion, and an extensive set of texts written on silk rolls, the famous *po-shu* manuscripts. Among the books found there are two slightly different copies of the *Tao Te Ching* and several other Taoist or Taoistic texts, some previously unknown. These are 350 years earlier than any other copies of the *Tao Te Ching* known to exist. Nonetheless they are several centuries later than the period to which the book is usually thought to have been written. They present many problems of interpretation. Yet they have already added greatly to our knowledge of early Taoism.

Some features of these early second-century B.C. manuscript copyings of the *Tao Te Ching* have invited far-ranging speculation. First of all the text is arranged with the *te* chapters placed ahead of the *tao* chapters, so this version of the book perhaps should be called the *Te Tao Ching*. Moreover the texts are about ten percent longer than the other versions that have been standard up to now, and they contain some variants of word and sentences making for differences of meaning. All those differences taken together seem to suggest that the emphasis is on the mundane and practical aspects of *te*, or how to gain results, so that some scholars see this version of the book as a handbook on politics. These two copies of the book in conjunction with related texts found with them have been interpreted by scholars in China as representing an amalgam of Legalist and Taoist ideas used to support the idea of a strongly activist, statist government. That would seem to be at the farthest possible reach from Taoist philosophy, but as we shall see in Chapter 7, this seemingly bizarre association of opposites was a feature of third- and second-century Legalist statecraft. In short these new finds greatly broaden our knowledge of early imperial political thought. Whether then they truly represent Taoism's earliest form—which seems quite unlikely—or are a subsequent corruption, is still speculative. The interest of many scholars has been drawn to these puzzles.

The *Tao Te Ching* is thus a strange combination of elements. On one level it is mere Taoist common sense about humans and the world. And on still another level it has been taken to be crafty political advice. For most of its serious students, however, it is mystical poetry trying to evoke a sense of something that cannot be put into words. Hence its language is purposefully ambiguous and indirect; it particularly utilizes paradox and bizarre juxtaposition to jolt people into thinking. A fellow student of the book notes:

> One reason for the multiplicity of translations—and more come out, year by year—is that the language of the *Tao Te Ching* is determinedly fascinating and frustrating. The protean quality of ancient Chinese language and the slipperiness of the concepts combine to give us a semantic object that is at once opaque and endlessly evocative. There is scarcely a sentence of which one can feel, "I've got it." Only perhaps after many rereadings does there emerge a very generalized sensation of what it all comes to, and this tends to limit the potential meanings we can attach to individual sentences—somewhat.
>
> The very first sentence informs us unmistakably that our chase for certainties is going to be a lively one. It contains six characters, three of them the same *tao*, which can mean "way, guide" (n., v.), "speak, practice" (n., v.), "reason" and many other things. By the time *Tao k'e tao fei ch'ang tao* has rolled over your tongue several times, it becomes appallingly clear that the meaning of *tao* is never going to remain docilely in any semantic slots. A colleague of mine once expressed himself as reasonably happy with the translation: "The Way that can be expressed is not the constant Way." So far as I know, none of the published translations have come up with precisely that; and it's a sensible translation—possibly the worst thing one could say about it. In any case, he is no longer satisfied with it.*

The *Tao Te Ching's* figures of speech and its rhythms of language are so artfully devised that it fixes itself in the mind and reemerges in everyone's speech. The book has cast a spell on Chinese culture that has persisted throughout the entire history of China, inducing learned people in every generation to study and prepare commentaries on it and countless numbers to ponder and memorize it. Its thought and its

---

* F. A. Kierman, Jr., in a private communication.

language have had as lasting and as pervasive an influence on the Chinese cultural experience as have Confucius and Mencius.

Chuang Tzu

Chuang Chou (ca. 369–286 B.C.), better known to us as the philosopher Chuang Tzu, is a fully historical person. Kings courted him, but he would not be defiled. Other philosophers debated with him, and he flailed them—somewhat humorously, for he did not really believe that arguments prove anything, although he enjoyed the sport. He had a brilliant mind and a truly magnificent command of language. He presented his ideas in philosophical essays full of fantasy and humor, touched with sardonic wit. They are compelling works of imagination that would have earned Chuang Tzu immortality in literature even if they had not been important as philosophy. They constitute a substantial work of thirty-one chapters, each an essay of ten or a dozen pages in English translation. Although some portions have been tampered with and added to by later persons, the core of the book is accepted by all scholars as authentic.

The ideas of the *Tao Te Ching* are Chuang Tzu's starting point, but he presents his thought much more extensively in essays written to be read as philosophic discourse. And the ideas themselves are more fully developed. Virtually every line of the *Tao Te Ching* is so ambiguous as to offer several superficially valid interpretations. In the *Chuang Tzu* we are seldom in doubt about the meaning of the single line, but we often are left guessing about the sense of a whole passage. Almost any part of the book may be taken literally or metaphorically, and then at any of several levels of metaphor.

As we have noted, a considerable problem for Taoism has been the vulgarization of its ideas by the literal-minded reader. When the elaborate metaphors necessary to project subtle concepts are misunderstood, the philosophy may be stood on its head. For example, Chuang Tzu talks a great deal about the necessity of man's nurturing his vital power, an idea already fixed in his time and associated with all kinds of physical exercises. There were dietary practices, physical stretchings and pullings, breath-control exercises leading to self-hypnosis, and sex techniques. Chuang Tzu utilizes the currency of these ideas to speak about another kind of "vital power," but he does not mean by that the vulgar notion of some means of overcoming nature, preserving life unnaturally, or achieving physical feats that ordinary man is not capable of. He ridicules the literal application of such techniques to achieve unnatural ends, but his ridicule is expressed in language so subtle that the simple-minded can quite misguidedly cite Chuang Tzu as the authority for their quite different view of the matter. Philosophical-minded Taoists have always understood that Chuang Tzu has only a philosophical purpose in mind, that he is interested only in mental clarity when he speaks of physical practices aiding concentration. The vulgarization of Taoism turned precisely on the point of whether one was to seek sagehood within nature or seek immortality and supernatural powers in defiance of nature. Although Chuang Tzu is clearly on the former path, his writings are not tracts for the masses, and he could do little to prevent the mass movement in the other direction. But he probably felt that each person has to seek the level of truth that is meaningful for him.

For himself and for those who could take the course he indicated, disciplining the body had no value in itself. He was neither yogi nor ascetic. Either of those approaches to life would have struck the Taoist mind as excessive and unnatural. But he was concerned with concentration, through which vision could be improved, ultimately to the point at which the *tao* is seen or experienced, and mystical knowledge is thus gained. The person who accomplished that became the true sage, the perfected person, the completely free and happy person.

Chuang Tzu's goal for humanity was happiness. Everything in his system of ideas except the concept of *tao* itself is relative. *Tao* is the only absolute, and it represents absolute freedom, absolute truth, absolute happiness. But relative freedom, relative truth, and relative happiness, as soon as we recognize them as merely relative, are nonetheless relatively valuable. Most Chinese felt that a wisdom was verified for them by Chuang Tzu even though they did not expect to attempt the mystic's personal verification of it for themselves. Hence Chuang Tzu's relative happiness and relative freedom were meaningful notions for everyone.

Taoism as applied philosophy for everyone forcefully projected the ideals of living simply in harmony with nature and doing no violence to one's own nature. At this level of application, relative standards of what is true, what is good, and what is beautiful can be accepted.

Confucians argued that these were absolutes and that moral relativism in particular compromised the very foundations of civilization. The Taoists agreed, but since they did not value civilization, the observation pleased them.

Nonetheless Taoism is practical; it recognizes the utility of getting along in the world which, for better or for worse, is a civilized world. The only danger was to take the human part of the world seriously as the Confucians did. When one takes distinctions seriously, he cuts reality into clearly distinguished parts; especially when the misguided knower reaches out to grasp "knowledge" external to himself, he separates "me" from "non-me," and that only confuses the mind. Partial reality is a contradiction in terms. The person who cannot see that may never be able to lose self by becoming one with the *tao*. And he will not only fail to achieve absolute happiness through recognizing his oneness with the absolute *tao*, but he is also very likely to be unable to gain a realistic perspective about things and achieve the relative happiness that comes from the simple Taoist life style in accord with nature.

Chuang Tzu's method is to seek to transcend distinctions and to detach oneself from immediate concerns. So this is true and that is false. Try to see them as points on a continuum extended to a circle. Do not disregard them. Relatively speaking, the ability to make such distinctions is what we call knowledge. Our purpose is not to deny knowledge, but to put it in its place so as to achieve greater knowledge. This greater knowledge is the product of disillusionment; but it is a post-knowledge, not the original ignorance, the infantile stupidity. The greater knowledge, paradoxically, is the greater stupidity. The Taoists value the idea of being "as if stupid," not being actually stupid. That is the greater stupidity which is defined by its opposite, as so many Taoist concepts are defined: the greater stupidity is the greater knowledge. When the Taoist learner learns to see through knowledge, which has to do only with the relative positions of things in the external world, he can then seek the absolute knowledge within himself.

These sound like simple, harmless ideals. In fact they are not so simple, nor did the Chinese whose interests lay with organized society and the strong state always regard them as harmless. Hsün Tzu said that Chuang Tzu was misled by his overwhelming conception of nature and failed to see humanity. Chuang Tzu went well beyond Lao Tzu in advocating not just laissez-faire government but complete anarchy. However it was the anarchy of the nonconforming individual. Chuang Tzu, "failing to see man," certainly did not believe in organization or in social movements. Hence his anarchism could not become a political threat, except that it gave a point of view to less-disinterested critics of the state. That relativist point of view and the battery of sardonic wit that went with it enables Taoist-inspired critics to convince people of the silliness of most public figures and all pompous roles. If one is trying hard to be a model governor or a high-minded minister, such needling can be hard to take.

Yet Chuang Tzu's delightfully malicious parodies of Confucius and his favorite disciples have always amused Confucian readers as well as everyone else. And the historical value of Taoism may be that it has served as a balance wheel on Confucianism. Whenever Confucians tended to go too far, to rigidify and petrify life with their standards and forms, to become overzealous in their ethical programs, Taoism helped to restore balance. Taoism in that sense has been, and one would hope still is, part of the built-in capacity for correction and renovation that has kept Chinese civilization so steadily on track.

Chapter Five
Mo Tzu: His Philosophical Ideas

Mo Tzu (ca. 479–438 B.C.) was the first important offshoot of the Confucian school. Born about the year that Confucius died, he must have studied under Confucian teachers contemporary with the sage's grandson but before the school had achieved its overwhelming prominence. After it achieved that, and especially after it became the official position of the Chinese empire in philosophy and education, dissidents tended to remain within the school, retaining the benefits that came from claiming Confucian correctness, content to establish divergent positions within the fold. Thus in later history there were no important offshoots from Confucianism who, like Mo Tzu, repudiated it and created their own new social philosophy.

We would expect to see similarities with the Confucians, and indeed, there are some; for example, seriousness of social commitment, the use of learning about the past to validate ideas, and a focus on governing to achieve moral ends. Nonetheless Mo Tzu disagreed strongly with certain essentials of Confucian teaching. He could not have been deterred from making a clean break with it. Although he had received something of the Confucian education, he developed his

own view of the ideal society and how to achieve it. And it is a view
very difficult to reconcile with either Confucian or contemporary Taoist values.

Mo Tzu (also spelled Moh Tzu, Motze, and sometimes Latinized as
Micius) is a fully historical personage, but one whose basic historical
identity is strangely lacking, even in a Chinese tradition thronged with
rather intangible characters. Mo may be his surname. His given name
is said to have been Ti, and there are several theories about the origins
and meanings of these appellations. Was Mo perhaps a title or an
adjective rather than a family name? Did it designate his class in
society, a trade, or a profession, such as that of a craftsman-builder,
or did it signify that he had been punished by branding on the fore-
head? All these are possible, derived from the meaning of mo: "black,
lampblack, ink, the dark mark of a brand or a tattoo." It has also long
been conjectured that Mo Tzu had a military background, that he
came from a family of the displaced knights who, as a class, were
disappearing in his time, forced to seek new roles in society and
suffering from sharp downward mobility. Mo Tzu's mind displays a
kind of military rigidity and simplifying tendency, a rather literal quality in its quest for intellectual order; and the society of his followers
became a rigorously organized order apparently modeled on military
prototypes. Moreover his followers, although holding fast to their
master's total repudiation of offensive warfare, became the acknowledged experts on defensive military tactics and technology in the
Warring States period, and as such played a prominent role in the
military history of the times. So the associations with the military are
numerous. Still it is not enough for us to conclude that Mo Tzu was
simply a disillusioned, jobless knight seeking the kind of ideal society
a military mind might conceive, for recent studies have advanced the
strong possibility that Mo Tzu was a craftsman-builder by trade, mo,
the lampblack used for measuring and marking timbers, being the
symbol of his professional guild. And in truth with these and several
other possible answers, the question must be left unsolved.

Yet in all these speculations about Mo Tzu's background, we see the
man as consistently identified with the middle and lower levels of his
society. His thought reeks of what we like to consider lower middle-
class virtues, and although when making that supercilious-sounding
observation, there are perhaps no meaningful analogies to any specific
Western social setting we may have in mind; nevertheless, it is sugges-

tive. Mo Tzu was obsessed with notions of profit and utility; in his system of ideas, what succeeds is therefore good. "Profit," it must be remembered, was the single word that most immediately aroused the ire of Mencius, and utility has never seemed a nice subject among inutile aristocrats.

Mo Tzu was likewise obsessed with a horror of waste and ostentatious consumption. His break with the Confucians seems to have been over the issue of ceremonies and rituals, which not only tended to maintain pompous aristocratic attitudes, but also—even worse—wasted material goods. Mo Tzu had absolutely no sympathy for foolishness like music, or notions like cosmic harmony, or any values associated with refinement of the mind and expression of the self. Mo Tzu called his followers to a hard and simple life in a manner very like what we might call old-fashioned Protestant evangelism. His rigid, inelastic social philosophy seemed barren and harsh to the critics of his own time, and it strikes us now as totally uncongenial to the tone and flavor of Chinese life, even the sterner Chinese life of today. Yet if one chooses to ignore the unattractive but (philosophically speaking) superficial barrier that the cultural poverty of Mo Tzu's private world sets up, one can then enter into a Mohist* intellectual world that is not without its intrinsic interest and historical importance.

Mo Tzu was the only native religious teacher that China ever had, it is customary to say. That of course excludes leaders of popular sects during the later imperial era, perhaps justifiable on the grounds that they have not left records of teachings that display original and highly developed religious ideas. Mo Tzu certainly did that. He formulated some religious ideas that are of considerable originality, apparently, in the Chinese setting. They seem to lack antecedents, and there are no later parallels to them. Mo Tzu's religion was one of gods and spirits, anthropomorphically conceived and literally believed in. We must assume that Mo Tzu developed these ideas within the framework of the commonly accepted Chinese cosmology; that is, Mo Tzu's gods and spirits were not creator-gods external to it because the issue is not one that had to be made explicit. But except for such points of shared intellectual ground, Mo Tzu's religious doctrines and those of his school are distinct from all others ever enunciated by any philosopher

* One is forced to hyphenate or use a conventional "h" to disyllabize the word—there is surely nothing "moist" about Mohism.

or teacher in Chinese history. Confucius' ethical system was built on secular foundations, as were all others; Mo Tzu alone needed gods to enforce his moral order. He believed in a supreme being which he called Heaven, or the Will of Heaven, which reigned throughout the universe like a king within his kingdom and who embodied the will that must inexorably punish evil and reward good. He believed quite literally and directly in a host of secondary supernatural beings who assisted that Heaven in enforcing the moral behavior of individuals and of governments. In his characteristically mechanical extension of all the implications, he also denounced the notion of fate as inconsistent with a purposive moral order. There can be no cosmic accidents or blind cosmic causes, and even the daily deeds of the little people must be fitted into the notion of a precisely rewarding and punishing Heaven. Mencius, it will be remembered, also stressed the role of heaven (meaning the natural order) in human affairs saying, "Heaven sees as the people see; heaven hears as the people hear." He conceived of heaven as a force responsive to the feelings and needs of people. Mo Tzu's Heaven was of another sort; knowing what humanity needed, it demanded that humans observe its authoritarian will.

Religion was necessary as the sanction for correct human behavior. But the Will of Heaven was not the sole cause of events in human lives. A person can be ill, as Mo Tzu said in explaining his own illness on one occasion, not necessarily only as a punishment for some bad act, certainly never as the result of blind fate, but often for quite natural reasons, such as the consequences of heat and cold, fatigue, or bad food. Mo Tzu was curiously realistic in his view of nature, while at the same time insisting on the supernatural. This combination is not unknown in our own tradition. Nor is his religious utilitarianism unfamiliar: Mo Tzu sounds much like Bentham and Mill. Although the West did not produce such a system of ideas until the eighteenth century, Mo Tzu in the fifth century B.C. enunciated a philosophy of universal love for the sake of everybody's profit.

Mo Tzu sought happiness for humans and told people that they must stir themselves energetically to achieve it, but he defined that happiness in narrowly material terms. His morality was also one of calculation: A thing is good if it demonstrably results in material benefits to all people equally. War is the greatest of evils because it is the most wasteful of life and treasure. Righteousness is simply the total abandonment of personal feelings that interfere with efficient productiveness and equitable distribution. Music and art are bad because they waste time and goods, divert energies, and neither feed nor clothe people. Confucian evil is a mere deflection from ethical harmony and not directly consequential, but Mohist evil is any deflection from positive productiveness, for that is offensive to Heaven who will directly punish it.

As Heaven loves all people equally, so man must do the same. Universal love (chien-ai) is the fundamental tenet of all Mohist doctrine. Mo Tzu probably took the Confucian ideal of jen (benevolence) and expanded on it, redefining it as a social quality of love (ai), an undifferentiating attitude of care for all humans alike. Yet it was the aspect of Mohism most shocking to the Confucian mind precisely because of its denial of family priorities. Mo Tzu's ideal may sound grander: Love all men equally. Then if all the sons in the whole world treat all old men as their fathers, a son need not show particular love and attention to his own father. But the Confucian ideal is undeniably closer to human expectations. The Confucian gradations of love and concern correspond to the ideal hierarchy of Confucian society. Likewise the Mohist ideal of universal love clearly implies Mohism's rigidly organized but egalitarian society. That sort of society could not be realized except through such organization.

For a period of perhaps two centuries, the Mohist organization flourished throughout many parts of China as "states within the states" of late Chou. It had its leader, the Chü-tzu or Supreme Head, who in theory achieved his position by general acknowledgment of his superior capacities, but who actually reached this pinnacle by working up the ladder of promotion in a central organization. In principle this worked about like the election of an American union leader. Having acknowledged a leader within a hierarchy of leadership, all followers were then bound to disciplined obedience. Within the Mohist organization, the leader's rules prevailed regardless of the laws of the state.

The economic communalism, denial of the family's special interests, and potential conflict with the state would all seem to place severe limits on organized Mohism's chances for survival. In fact, however, it may have suffered most from yet another of its special virtues. It may be that its role in defending states against the irresistible aggressor who between 229 and 221 B.C. crushed the last of the Warring States is what simultaneously caused the disappearance of Mohism; the Ch'in conquest may have decimated the Mohist communities as it conquered one after another of the states that sought in vain to defend themselves against Ch'in's invincible armies. Some scholars have raised the intriguing suggestion that lingering Mohist influences were responsible for the phenomenon of "knights errant" in the early imperial centuries. Robin Hood-like individuals and bands of men who lived beyond the law but who seemed to have some social consciousness may have drawn their guiding principles from Mo Tzu's school of thought. But we can only speculate on such connections; all we can state with certainty is that the Mohist writings remained, but no Mohist school survived; and until a revival of interest in the texts as objects of philological study in the eighteenth century, Mohism was virtually lost to Chinese civilization.

In summary we must conclude that the most aberrant feature of Mohism within the intellectual and cultural milieu of early China was its failure to accommodate to some basic psychological factors. It displayed no awareness of natural human feelings and their influence on the way societies work. In the ancient anti-Mohist critiques of most telling significance, Mohism was "contrary to the hearts of all men," as Chuang Tzu put it. Mohism's use of history was also strange in that most historical-minded of cultures. History was inescapably important, but Mohist's sought validation of their views by going back to the most ancient of periods, the Hsia dynasty, which tradition held had preceded the Shang. The more mythical the period, the more susceptible it was to the uses of a literal-minded fundamentalism; but by that very fact, the less convincing was it in an age of increasing rationalism and in competition with more pertinent, more recent historical lessons. Confucius, in contrast, made his historical points with the material of the more nearly contemporary Chou era.

Furthermore, running directly counter to all the developmental trends of the age, the Mohists rejected the free and natural workings of social process, social mobility, and political growth. They insisted on an artificially structured organization that had neither the glamour of ancient aristocratic ideals nor the satisfactions of the new social freedoms. And despite all the obvious shortcomings of a Confucianism practiced deficiently by petty-minded bureaucrats and would-be aristocrats posing as "superior men," Confucianism's suspended judgment and nondoctrinaire ethics had inevitably a wider appeal and greater effectiveness than the simplistic formulas of the Mohists. Mohism, as social doctrine especially, deserved to disappear; it had little to offer a rich civilization.

Nevertheless Mohism seemed to hold a special message for Chinese in the nineteenth and twentieth centuries, and it has seen a curious revival of importance in the intellectual heritage of modern China. It appealed to Christian missionaries and to those influential Chinese modernizers who were influenced by Christian and Western thought, because its doctrine of universal love seemed akin to Christian doctrine. Early missionaries sometimes used this Chinese precedent to make modern Chinese pagans take Christian love seriously and to validate an outlandish doctrine by showing that respectable ancient Chinese had said something not dissimilar. The modern Chinese study of Mohism has undoubtedly been largely associated with Chinese Christian circles. Modern revolutionaries too were attracted to Mohism because the idea of universal love seemed a useful tool in breaking down the family-centered attitudes that they considered the major bar to social change.

Both these uses of Mohism in our time are in fact somewhat specious. Yet there is another aspect of Mohism that deserves our attention as historians of Chinese thought. That is its epistemology, Mohism's major contribution to classical Chinese philosophy—its consideration of the problem of how humans know.

Chapter Six
The Problem of Knowledge

After the death of Mo Tzu, his topical essays, probably the first formal essays of philosophical discourse to be written in China, continued to provide his followers with material for debate. Mohists were soon famous as skilled opponents of all the debaters representing the many competing philosophical positions. There is a kind of symmetry in the fact that in the contentious arts of the tongue as well as those of the sword, the Mohists became technical virtuosos in the frustration of opposing initiatives. They assiduously reworked their founder's arguments, often restating them in variant forms. Some chapters of the book, *The Mo Tzu,* exist in three variously reworked versions. They also added a considerable body of material that continued the development of Mo Tzu's original doctrines.

Knowledge in the Mohist School

Some of the later additions to *The Mo Tzu,* as we know it today, become quite specifically involved with problems of an epistemological nature and with problems of formal logic; that is, the Mohists tried to develop a theory of knowledge to explain how we know what we know and what standards can be applied to judge its validity. They also became interested in the formal ways in which correct statements can be made and in the means of verifying the accuracy of such propositions. These concerns, central to classical Greek and to Western philosophy in general, never became separate divisions of Chinese philosophy. Their methods were not very extensively developed, and their results were not highly valued. As formal exercises they remained peripheral to the concerns and values of China's major philosophical schools, even though as issues they were necessarily of concern in any systematic, reflective thinking about life.

Confucius had been the first to show an interest in the problem of knowledge, which to him was essentially the problem of the quest for certainty. Implicit in his system of ideas is the notion that human wisdom, guided by civilization's ethical concepts, which in themselves reflected basic human nature, provides whatever certainty we are capable of attaining. The applications mattered more to him, however, than did ways of testing verbal formulations. This is what a leading modern historian of Chinese philosophy, Fung Yu-lan, means when he states that for Confucius the problem of knowledge held only ethical significance and that in Confucianism it did not become a problem of logic per se until it was taken up by Hsün Tzu.

It was in the doctrine of the rectification of names that Confucius expressed his formulation of the problem of knowledge; it had the very important consequence of introducing the issue of how name and reality, or term and content, are related. It forced philosophers to be aware that discrepancies could occur, and in that way must have led to speculation about the knowing process. Again, however, the emphasis is on the social and ethical implications of how accurately terms correspond to content, not on the more abstract problems either of how man knows things or of how he verifies the soundness of his statements.

If, as we think, the *Tao Te Ching* represents Lao Tzu and the early Taoists, it shows them anxious simply to expose the limited nature of what the world called knowledge. For them the relativity of truth was evident as soon as a human-centered vision was corrected by the larger view of nature, and this somewhat disparaged the quest for ordinary truth. They did, to be sure, posit the existence of a greater knowledge; but it could only be experienced intuitively, not known objectively. Hence no truly accurate statements about it were possible; checks on the soundness of statements about it could not acquire more than the limited significance of a word game. The early Taoists could therefore make no contribution to formal logic, and their epistemology could not very well be shared with other thinkers.

The Mohists, however, could contribute something new and highly important. They could do this because, unlike the Taoists, they believed that intellectual certainty was both attainable and expressible, and, unlike the Confucians, they believed that argument per se possessed high utility in ascertaining truth and was therefore intrinsically valuable. In their literal-minded manner, they granted to debate a function that ethics-oriented Confucians derided: "Contentious words," Confucians said, "merely shift the attention from the fundamental to the superficial, make people tricky and disputatious, and damage social harmony."

The later Mohists of the fourth and third centuries B.C. thus did not have many opportunities to engage leading Confucians and Taoists in debate, but they did have many other worthy opponents. This Golden Age of philosophy has also been called the Period of the Hundred Schools. Philosophizing flourished. Innumerable schools must have existed, though now we know only the thought of very few, and perhaps very few deserve a permanent place in history. The problem of knowledge is but one key to the character of these schools, but it is the one that we shall employ here in making our bows to some other aspects of early China's intellectual history. The aspects that key particularly opens to us are those of sophistry, logic, and philosophies relying heavily on techniques of debate. We know these early epistemologists and logicians from no complete texts, only from quotations of their leading arguments in the texts transmitted by their opponents. Thus the record is neither complete nor fair. What it reveals is tantalizing, because it looks as if the Chinese Ming-chia (School of Names or Nominalists) and Pien-che (literally "debaters" or Dialecticians) included logicians of importance and high competence. The fragments indicate that the capacity for development along these lines in Chinese philosophy clearly existed. Why then, since we regard this as something of central importance to philosophy, did that development not take place and become of equal importance to Chinese philosophy?

That is an example of the culturally parochial question. The answer will be of great interest to us, and we have a right to ask it, but if pursued to its limits, it will lead us astray from the main concerns of Chinese cultural history. The first stage of the answer is simply that the Chinese looked into formal logic and found it less important than other concerns in philosophy. The further stages of the answer may be more appropriately directed to the reasons why *our* civilization finds traditional logic centrally important rather than why the Chinese or some other peoples did not; that is, the assumption that the familiar is the norm from which variations demand special explanation is parochial. Likewise any unconscious but implicit universalizing from culturally parochial ground tends to become frustratingly irrelevant.

Let us therefore take the Chinese logicians as evidence relevant to the Chinese world of thought. Speculation about other dimensions of their philosophies, especially suggestions about their metaphysical theories, are particularly intriguing. But because no one has been able to make a completely convincing reconstruction of what those might have comprised, our interest in them can go little beyond noting their stimulus to other thinkers, particularly in relation to the problem of knowledge and the attitudes of the other schools toward the technical mastery of argument they possessed.

Whether the Mohist contribution to logic and epistemology is attributable to other schools or to the Mohists themselves is difficult to ascertain; it was, in any event, the outgrowth of their interaction. The Mohists became deeply involved in questions about the sources of knowledge, uses of names, and methods of inference, and always showed a preference for common-sense attitudes. But they subjected their opponents' tricky rebuttals to searching analysis, trying to extend the reliability of common sense and always looking for practical utility. They were not interested in knowledge simply as the product of teaching, for they had a utilitarian objection to the luxury of humanistic study for general liberal arts purposes. Nor could they, in their plebeian skepticism about the revelations of their learned superiors, simply accept knowledge as a corpus of given facts. They had to know where it came from and what it would be used for. So they invented, or at least used, the following analysis of the knowing experience and the elements involved in it.

Knowledge means a knowing faculty, that by which one knows but which is not itself knowledge, for example, the eye.

Knowledge means meeting, in which the knowing faculty meets the
object and registers an impression, for example, seeing.

Knowledge means understanding, which results from the knowing
faculty reflecting on the object and thereby knowing clearly.

Thus they recognized three constituent parts of knowledge: the knowing faculty, the contact with the object of knowledge, and reflection
or understanding.

This corresponds rather closely to our psychological analysis of
three constituents of knowledge: the sense organ, the object, and
ratiocination. In terms of epistemology, the first and the third elements
are those of sense perception and of reasoning in the knower, and the
second is the known. All must exist before there can be knowledge.

But what was the value of defining these parts of ordinary experience? To the Mohists this simplification and clarification of the problem had the value of reassuring persons about the soundness of their
common sense and of warding off the sophistic extremes and confusing
paradoxes of the professional word jugglers. Thus they also went on
to classify knowledge by the means known.

Hearing—knowledge received through verbal transmission (including
words read), such as all historical knowledge.

Inference—knowledge that extends from that directly acquired through
our senses to that which cannot be directly perceived. For this the
Mohists used the word "duration," saying, for example, that we
know the blue of an object elsewhere by the duration or extension of
the concept "blue" from a blue object experienced directly to an
object conceived as existing beyond our perception.

Personal experience—all knowledge ultimately derives from this, since
all perceived and inferred knowledge depends on some relation with
experience to be meaningful; that is, general knowledge of a thing is
not known from being told its name, but is known from having
perceived some members of the category to which the new
thing-name applies.

We might well object that all three classifications of knowledge are, in
fact, reducible, according to the varying ways they are obtained, to the
third. By regarding them as three classes, the Mohists showed that
their epistemology was limited by their practical interests in applying
it. Yet they must be credited with systematic and often rather perceptive efforts.

After classifying knowledge by the three ways it can be gained, they also classified it into four categories according to the type of knowledge itself.

names (to be further subdivided according to type)
actualities—the things names apply to
correspondences—knowledge of how the preceding two types pair up to constitute further knowledge
action—involving will and movement, knowledge about how to do certain things

These are interesting categories. The first seems to correspond to what the modern logician would call the logic of terms, the second to the logic of classes, and the third to the logic of function or predication. The fourth, strictly speaking, is not a logical category but not a surprising inclusion in the list for practical-minded Mohists to have insisted upon.

The Mohists also devised seven ways of establishing a statement or seven kinds of proof derived from the form in which propositions are made. So simplified a discussion of the subject does not indicate the scope and quality of the Mohists' involvement, but it may be enough to display the intensity with which the followers of Mo Tzu sharpened the tools of debate so as to defend the master's ideas and to achieve clear-cut order in the world of words.

Hui Shih and Kung-sun Lung

Among all the famous logicians of the Nominalist and Dialectician schools, the names of Hui Shih, also called Hui Tzu (ca. 380–305 B.C.), and his contemporary, Kung-sun Lung, are the best known. A separate work called the *Kung-sun Lung Tzu* exists, though its text is very corrupt; perhaps its set of twenty-one paradoxes and the discussions of "white horse is not horse"* and other similar statements are genuine. Hui Shih's set of ten paradoxes and some other statements attributed to him are included in the *Chuang Tzu*, but Hui Shih's own

---

* A famous bit of early Chinese sophistry designed to confuse the opponent about the extension of categories such as "white" and "horse."

arguments accompanying them are not preserved. The two sets of paradoxes consist of superficially incongruous statements much like—in some cases curiously identical with—those of the Greek philosopher, Zeno the Eleatic (490–430 B.C.), but there is no suggestion of a common source of both. For example:

> Kung-sun Lung:
> At times an arrow in flight is neither moving nor still.
> A foot-rule cut in half every day will still partly remain even after being halved daily throughout ten thousand generations.
>
> Zeno:
> A flying arrow is really at rest.
> To reach any point, a moving body must first reach the halfway mark, and so forth.

Paradox is the obvious and most useful tool of the debater, and it has a long history in early China. The paradoxes of these debaters, like those of Greek thinkers, have unexpected but in fact self-evident and common-sense justifications when cleverly argued. In contrast, however, the famous paradoxes of the Book of Changes are not so simply dealt with, nor are those that the Taoists used.

Yet as a subject in modern study of early Chinese thought, Hui Shih's and Kung-sun Lung's two sets of paradoxes and the intellectual movements of which they are the manifestation have attracted much serious attention. There are hints that these are more than mere debaters' tricks, that they form part of larger systems of metaphysics and ethics. For example, Hui Shih's tenth paradox—Love all things equally: The universe is one—suggests Mohism's doctrine of universal love and also the Taoist relativity of all things, as well as a mystical monism. Both sets seem to be concerned with demonstrating that there is only one time and one space which are (is) continuous, infinitely divisible, and constantly changing, and that all perception of the cosmos is relative to the perceiver in ways that make many common-sense statements about what is perceived only relatively true. Yet they are not Taoist because they apparently believed that argument can cut through the relativist confusions and reach the solid ground of verified objective truth. Moreover other aspects of their philosophies probably varied widely. Hui Shih argued with Chuang Tzu; they obviously enjoyed crossing swords, and they clearly stood on opposite sides of some basic philosophic issues of their time. But we have great difficulty in filling in Hui Shih's side of those, so rather than attempt a hypothetical reconstruction of his or other logicians' systems of philosophy, let us merely examine how they contributed to the developing solutions of epistemological problems.

Among the twenty-one paradoxes that are attributed to "the dialecticians of the world" (in *Chuang Tzu*, xxxiii) and that Hui Shih thought important, but that are explained at some length in the book of *Kung-sun Lung Tzu* (we do not really know just whose ideas they are), are these two: Fire is not hot, and The eye does not see. The discussion of the first of these establishes an important epistemological concept about the object "fire" and the relationship to it of the quality "hot." The first is a universal that exists apart from our perception, but the second is subjective, existing in our sensation, and is therefore descriptive of our awareness and not of the object "fire" itself.

"The eye does not see" adds a fourth component to the Mohists' three-phase analysis of the knowing process. The discussion in the *Kung-sun Lung Tzu* says:

> Whiteness is beheld by the eye, but the eye sees by means of light. However, light does not have the faculty of vision. Then, neither light nor the eye can by itself see whiteness. It must be the mind that sees it. But the mind alone cannot see it either. Thus, the sight of whiteness is something separate from whiteness itself.

Here four factors—whiteness, the eye, light, and the mind—are held to be necessary to seeing. This introduces the new factor of light, adding it to the three elements that the Mohists were already aware of.

These logicians were performing an epistemological analysis that led to the discovery of the problem of things and their attributes. Their starting point and their attitudes toward the problem are not unlike those of British empiricism, and we might read a bit of Hobbes or even more of Hume into these theories of knowledge in ancient Chinese thought. Hui Shih was on the track of some important ideas, but his contemporaries commented that he had an interest only in confounding others' arguments, not in projecting any system of ideas of his own. Whether that is true or not, it is a strange and perhaps a sad thing that other thinkers did not follow through and produce systematic epistemology and ontology from these beginnings. Part of the reason no one did so, clearly, is that the replies from Chuang Tzu, and later from Hsün Tzu—regardless of their objective, intrinsic value as philosophy—were overwhelmingly effective in discouraging the Chinese from considering this line of thought as significant or valuable.

Chuang Tzu

Chuang Tzu was as brilliantly perceptive as Hui Shih; in addition he believed in something that he could make very meaningful to his audience. He believed in showing that a higher certainty was attainable and that, being basically unrelated to "the five paths" of the senses, it did not concern the awareness of external objects in a dichotomy of the knower and the known. Hence he shifts the focus from How do we know what? to How one can know all/nothing confidently? He added an element to the discussion of how man knows; he called it the "light of reason." This term is derived from the Mohists' and Dialecticians' use of the idea of light—that by which things are seen. But Chuang Tzu's "light of reason" is not the light perceived by the eye, nor is his "reason" the ratiocination referred to by those other philosophers. Chuang Tzu's "reason" is the tao itself. For him true knowledge does not come from any exercise of a person's intellectual faculties to reflect on sensory experience, to lend pattern and meaning to the impressions conveyed by the natural senses. Rather, knowledge of the kind he is most interested in consists in the sudden dawning of a light that reestablishes the continuum including knower and known and the tao; it is the mystical experience in which knower and known become, or become aware that they are, one.

Hence for Chuang Tzu the problem of this and that, or the problem of how terms and attributes are to be delimited, leads one in precisely the wrong direction. Classifying or limiting knowledge fractures the greater knowledge. All the logicians' paradoxes were invitations to argue about just those limits. The professional debaters' ability to confuse the average person by juggling these limits was to the Taoists no more than an exhibition of sophistry. Chuang Tzu and all the Taoists also spoke in paradoxes, but with an entirely different purpose and attitude. Some roughly parallel passages from Hui Shih and Chuang Tzu illustrate this.

Hui Shih:
The heavens are as low as the earth; the mountains are as low as the marshes. [This is a logical issue involving things and their attributes. We expect "heavens" and "mountains" to designate high things, but Hui Shih would invoke cases of clouds ("heavens") being seen below the tops of mountains ("earth") and of marshes being found high on mountain tops.]

Chuang Tzu:
In all the world there is nothing larger than the tip of a hair; the great Mount T'ai is small. [These paradoxes are not to be dissolved by citing peculiar exceptions to the expected norms, but metaphysically, on the level of the identity and indivisibility of all things.]

Hui Shih:
The sun at noon is the sun declining; the creature born is the creature dying.

Chuang Tzu:
Where there is life there is death; where there is death there is life [In this pair of statements the differences in intent scarcely need be pointed out.]

Hui Shih:
Love all things equally, for the heavens and the earth are one composite body. [One faces a logical inability to delimit the "this" and the "that" consistently and accurately.]

Chuang Tzu:
The universe and I were produced together and all things and I are one. [There is a transcendental identity in the mystically experienced tao.]

These examples suggest that Hui Shih had the rather mundane purpose of challenging our common sense by manipulating terms and meanings. Chuang Tzu produced paradoxes for the psychological purpose of jolting the imagination, casting doubt on objective knowledge, and convincing people that by going in another direction, they could reach a higher clarity. We may argue that this harmed Chinese thought, because philosophy was turned away from developing the purely intellectual tools for verifying statements and toward other, wholly subjective ways of finding certainty. But Chuang Tzu did not have the last word among the preimperial thinkers on this subject.

Hsün Tzu did. And although he repudiated Chuang Tzu's subjective idealism, he did not strengthen the cause of objective or empirical epistemology.

Hsün Tzu

As the spokesman in his time for Confucian thought, Hsün Tzu had to show the fallacy of the logicians' sophistry as well as repudiate the socially irresponsible Taoist arguments of Chuang Tzu. Taking up the problem of knowledge, he developed Confucius' rectification-of-names idea to the status of an important concept in formal logic and in epistemology.

Hsün Tzu examined and accepted the four-phase analysis of the act of knowing, which we have illustrated by "whiteness," "the eye," "light," and "the mind." But he added other factors and suggested here something like Kant's *apperception,* that is, the mind's consciousness of itself as a knowing object. The Mohists had said, "Knowledge is a meeting," meaning that the mind must reflect on or react to sensory perception before it becomes knowledge. Hsün Tzu refined this, noting that, although sensory perception can supply a mere meeting, there are other conditioning factors that affect knowledge at that moment. The mind is a classifying agent; it classifies impressions and makes distinctions among them. True knowledge consists in the ability to do that accurately. Hence he developed a systematic terminology for relating such classifications, ranging from the most general classes to the most specific. After establishing standards for judging the accuracy of that classifying activity, he went on to analyze a number of psychological factors that determine the quality of the mind's efforts to achieve knowledge. A wavering attentiveness to perception may affect its quality; emotional factors of prejudice or passion may distort perception or classification. Here is a great beginning in epistemological and psychological inquiry. In its psychological sensitivity, it is typical of Confucianism in particular and Chinese thought in general. But it is also typical that Confucians regarded this as important only as applied philosophy—and they applied it to pedagogy. As an abstract inquiry into a theory of knowledge, they carried it no further.

But Hsün Tzu *did* believe in the usefulness of terms and in the importance of the ideas they conveyed. So he also responded to the logical paradoxes of Hui Shih, though without resorting to Chuang Tzu's relativism and subjectivity. To him as a Confucian, relativism implied ethical irrelevance, and it was abhorrent. As a systematic and clear-minded thinker, he found the necessity to maintain distinctions of prime importance. And as a philosopher of culture, he saw names and terms as one of man's greatest and most essential inventions.

Hsün Tzu would never identify the *logos* with god; to him words exemplified *man* at his most practical and intelligent. They are, he said, the arbitrary invention of man and have no meaning except as people agree on them. The social force of agreement gives words their validity and usefulness; there is no necessary relationship between name and reality. Hence when setting forth a paradox such as "the highest mountain is not high," a dialectician is merely violating social convention, not adducing any new idea. Hsün Tzu's answer to such insidious nonsense was to invoke his system of terms, arranged to show the hierarchies from most general to most specific, with which he analyzed three kinds of formal fallacies inherent in the improper use of names. Through these formulas he could deal handily with all the paradoxes that involved humankind's rational perception of useful knowledge. And he saw no reason to be much interested in any other kind.

Implications of Chinese Epistemology

Were we to review all the other known philosophies of the Golden Age, we would find in most of them practical concern for the problem of order in society, efforts to establish theories of human nature, and philosophic justifications for particular patterns of living. We would find but little speculation just for speculation's sake. China had a distinct dearth of "pure philosophers" who spun out theories about abstract philosophical issues. But as the foregoing discussions of Mohism and the logicians show, some ancient Chinese thinkers did consider the formal problems of logic and had the ability to deal with epistemological issues in a fairly advanced and sophisticated manner. The lack of further development in China, therefore, reflects a choice.

Yet Chinese thought had its characteristic mode, one that was quite different from the modes of classical Greek, ancient Indian, and other notable early philosophic traditions. What caused China's distinctiveness? Is the "cosmological gulf" between China and the rest of the world (discussed in Chapter 2), if it can be considered fully established, sufficient explanation of all these further points of distinctiveness? Or is the cosmological gulf itself merely part of a cultural set, the whole of which demands more fundamental explanation of its distinctiveness, or of its Chineseness?

Coupled with the characteristic mode of Chinese thought, as illustrated in its handling of the problem of knowledge, are several other distinctive features of Chinese intellectual history. Many scholars have noted these, and some have attempted to formulate explanations based on comparisons with Western intellectual history. Joseph Needham has observed certain cases in the history of Chinese mathematical and astronomical sciences where the ancient Chinese adopted solutions conceptually quite different from, but not necessarily scientifically inferior to, those adopted in the West. Chinese mathematics was from its beginnings more algebraic, whereas Greek mathematics was more geometric in character. Again Chinese astronomy was polar and equatorial in conception and method, whereas Western astronomy was ecliptic. Wolfram Eberhard quotes Needham: "If, like all Chinese science, Chinese astronomy was fundamentally empirical and observational, it was spared the excesses and aberrations, as well as the triumphs, of Occidental theorizing."*

We may also observe that the development of epistemological and metaphysical theory in classical Greek thought came after a prior interest in and development of mathematics. Pythagoras antedated Socrates by a century and a half. In China the great interest in and development of mathematics occurred in the Han dynasty, some centuries after the Golden Age of philosophy had more or less fixed the characteristic mode in thought. So the sequence of these developments was reversed. But does this observation explain anything?

The Polish historian of Chinese thought, Januz Chmielewski, notes a preoccupation with the concept and significance of nonidentity in early Chinese logic; this contrasts in his mind with Greek logicians' functionally analogous but qualitatively different focus on the concept of identity, as in the syllogism.

---

* Quoted in Wolfram Eberhard's review of Needham's work, *Journal of Asian Studies* 19 (November 1959): 65.

Throughout this book we have stressed the perceptiveness of psychological observation and the unifying preoccupation with the psychological element in almost all early Chinese schools of thought. All these generalized observations *display* the distinctiveness of Chinese thought. What, however, do they contribute to *explaining* that distinctiveness? Moreover do they bear in any way on the generally noted Chinese preference for the practical, the applied aspects of philosophy as opposed to the more theoretical approach of Western philosophy?

While it by no means offers a comprehensive or wholly satisfactory explanation of what makes Chinese thought distinctive, the fact that all schools of Chinese thought have looked with great suspicion upon the concern with any purely speculative theory of knowledge disputatiously maintained (was the association of theory and dispute necessary?) must have acted as a major deterrent to the development of such fields of inquiry, and that constriction must be judged to have affected the profile of Chinese thought markedly. At the same time, this unwillingness to argue about theory displays further the characteristic mindset of the early Chinese intellectual world; it is in the pattern. We have noted that Confucius' doctrine of the rectification of names had only ethical, not theoretical or epistemological intent.

Similarly among later thinkers, any concern which did not prove *useful* in immediate application tended to be rejected. Chuang Tzu said: "If we look at Hui Shih's ability from the standpoint of Heaven and Earth, it was only like the restless activity of a mosquito or gadfly; of what service was it to anything?" Hsün Tzu, who went further than any other Confucian in sharpening the tools of thinking, nonetheless noted that Hui Shih's teachings "could not serve as the basis for government" and that he "worked much but accomplished little." He concluded that Hui Shih was "blinded by phrases and didn't know realities." The historian Ssu-ma T'an of the second century B.C., although somewhat sympathetic toward Taoism and therefore not so relentlessly practical-minded as the typical orthodox Confucians, complained that Hui Shih "lost sight of human feelings." In the second century A.D., the great Confucian scholar and historian, Pan Ku, though acknowledging that "correct names" are important and that in fact the search for them had been started by Confucius, nevertheless added that, when the search becomes disputatious, it creates only division and disorder. With him, as characteristically with all later Confucians, order and practical social good were more important in any philosophy than a search for abstract truth.

So one implication we can clearly derive as we review the problem of knowledge is that the cultural values of the civilization are thoroughly intertwined with the development of its intellectual history. Another is that we can describe much more than we can explain at this stage in our knowledge of early China. The characteristic mode is clear; its causes, much less so.

Chapter Seven
The Creation of the Chinese Empire

To many readers of history, including many Chinese readers of their own history, China of the last hundred years looks disturbingly like China in the century from about 300 to 200 B.C. In that century the era of protracted civil war called the Warring States period ended. The denouement was still more unpleasant: political consolidation to be sure, but under the harshest of regimes. In the violence and frustration, the values of the old civilization seemed to have been swallowed up. A century of chaos had apparently allowed a political movement—one that combined unbeatable military force and psychologically apt organizational techniques—to impose itself upon the entire Chinese world. After coming to power in 221 B.C., the revolutionary new regime, the Ch'in dynasty, fundamentally altered the structure of society and government; controlled cultural life in unprecedented depth and detail; managed the economy; imposed reforms on the language and standardized its writing system, weights, measures, coinage, and even the gauges of vehicles and roads; and mobilized the masses of the people for vast building projects.

Confronting the awesome similarity to more recent events, some take comfort in noting that the Ch'in dynasty was brief; others observe gloomily how profoundly and permanently it altered Chinese life in its short span. In the last analysis, however, the political events of two thousand years ago defy any real analogy to those of our own time, no matter how tempting the parallels become. This is as true of China's as of other histories. To be sure, Chinese civilization displays a unique continuity; yet the level of culture, the structure of society, the form and functioning of government, the degree and scope of possible change—even the people's expectations of their government—have all changed drastically in the past twenty-two centuries. Perhaps the only constant among all these variables is human nature itself, and we cannot even demonstrate that to be true. Comparisons we must make, for history is by its nature comparative. Yet comparisons assuming significant underlying analogy run into serious trouble when they are examined closely. As we talk about the Ch'in, let us not seem to be telling fables about the present, for the Ch'in experience helps us understand modern China as one component of its substance, not as its long-drawn shadow.

Ch'in institutional innovations were very important to Chinese history; some of the basic forms created then had only to be reconstituted from time to time by later regimes establishing new dynasties. The Ch'in government was the first organically centralized administration that China had known; yet its experiment in installing and maintaining a centrally controlled bureaucratic administration was based on only about a century of experience in the province-sized state of Ch'in itself. This political innovation, however, accompanied and reflected fundamental social changes then underway throughout the Chinese world. China was at the point of transition from a system of closed classes and a bound tenant peasantry to one of independent landowning farmers in a society no longer having a legally privileged elite of hereditary status. The state of Ch'in, and finally the dynasty of Ch'in, became the instrument for hastening this process of social development and formally establishing it first within its own area and then throughout the Chinese cultural realm. And politically, although the state of Ch'in took advantage of a general expectation that all states and regions within the Chinese cultural realm should and inevitably would be united into one political entity (as they had theoretically been under the Western Chou almost a thousand years earlier), its practical accomplishment was indeed a new thing in Chinese history. No subsequent government has had to face that problem in that way again. Thus the internal dynamics of the political process by which Ch'in rose and fell in the space of a few decades were in important ways very special to that time in history.

True, we can cite features of Ch'in history that offer attractive analogies for use by the student of recent Chinese history. But to say that its measures were Draconian and its ideology quite incompatible either with the Great Tradition or popular sentiment, and to note that it was consequently overthrown by desperate masses who would no longer tolerate its existence, is merely to raise a number of accurately but only superficially descriptive features of Ch'in rule. It does not necessarily follow that they bear any essential relationship to each other or explain the process of rise and fall of regimes in history, then or later, for they involve no explicit analysis, and they prove no specific issues of cause and effect.

Most interestingly that superficial kind of comparison of Ch'in with the present ignores the issue of ideological and institutional origins. The Ch'in system of government was wholly a product of Chinese civilization, the same civilization that produced Confucius and Mencius, the Taoists and the Mohists, and all the rest. Although the forms of Ch'in government and military organization involved significant interaction with the barbarians of the northwest border areas, a geographical factor especially important in the rise and the heritage of Ch'in, Ch'in government was a response of Chinese civilization to those conditions, not a borrowing of non-Chinese elements. Chinese civilization then, as for two thousand years thereafter until the nineteenth century, was, if we discount for the moment the eventual Buddhist component, essentially an intramural civilization. It consistently generated within itself the essential elements of any new cultural and institutional mix that might develop. Since the nineteenth century, however, the cultural monism of the Chinese world has been battered down irrevocably. China has become a contributor to and recipient of the world's intellectual currents. The fact that many intellectual and cultural elements of present-day China originated elsewhere may be of primary importance in explaining their essential character, and that further complicates any analogies of ancient past to present.

Let us set this issue aside and focus upon the historical backgrounds of Legalism—the doctrines with which the Chinese empire was forged. We will attempt to understand how such ideas could have been spawned by the antilegalistic, humanistic, and hitherto tradition-minded civilization of early China. For the startling thing about the Ch'in political and cultural system is that it was narrowly and rigor-ously legalistic, statist in a way that expressly denied all humanistic values, and quite implacable in its scorn for venerated tradition.

Where are we to find the roots for these un-Chinese elements? Or is it the word "un-Chinese" that we must reexamine here? In point of fact, there is no single component of the Ch'in system that is not wholly indigenous, yet the word "un-Chinese" reflects the unvarying Chinese assessment of the Ch'in experiment. Ch'in, the "un-Chinese," represents everything that the Chinese expressly did not wish to be thereafter, according to the way their Confucian Great Tradition had crystallized what they should aspire to and what they should turn away from. The vigor of that Great Tradition in keeping its alternate ideal meaningful to Chinese, utilizing "the faults of Ch'in" (which became a favorite topic for political and social essays in the following Han dynasty) to illustrate its points, has meant that, on the level of ideology, Ch'in Legalism was abhorrently un-Chinese. No philoso-pher, statesman, or tyrant thereafter could ever openly espouse Ch'in tactics or Legalist doctrines. Yet at the same time, it was Ch'in institu-tions that had made the unified Chinese empire possible, and they could not be wholly abandoned without also abandoning the struc-tural basis of national unity.

So for the two thousand years of post-Ch'in imperial Chinese his-tory, the Chinese state has in fact lived with and become quite adjusted to the dilemma of being something that it could not openly proclaim and defend. Comparable dilemmas are not unknown elsewhere in history. But we must recognize its existence here both to explain the wholly Chinese nature of the Ch'in emergence and to clarify the limitations and contradictions implicit in such terms as "imperial Con-fucianism" and "the Confucian state." Chinese civilization is not inaccurately called Confucian, for the Confucian current in its intellec-tual and cultural life was indeed the mainstream. Yet the institutions of the imperial era were not produced out of Confucian experience or on Confucian ideal models (though, as we have noted, the Hsün Tzu strand of Confucian thought is by no means as difficult to accommo-date to imperial realities as the others). The Chinese imperial system, both in its structure and its ideology, is an example of the tension between actual and ideal patterns. The ideal was subjectively identified as "Confucian," and the actual was, by our objective analysis, Legalist in origin and was only gradually modified by somewhat superficially imposed Confucian influences at first, as well as by many other components of popular culture. And even as these merged through the long centuries, the Confucian compromise with forms and forces that denied or limited its ideals was ever to remain just that. It has been difficult for modern scholars to judge whether this is evidence of the fatal weakness of Confucianism or of the greatness of viable compromise, but the latter seems to say more.

Throughout the early imperial centuries when the form of the Chinese state was becoming established, a wide range of historical forces was also causing cultural growth and further institutional adaptation. Problems had to be met, and government had to be adjusted to new realities that neither the Confucian theorists of the Warring States period nor the Legalists of the Ch'in era had anticipated, and for which neither had supplied precise ready-made solutions. Yet the Confucians and their Legalist opponents had very largely contributed the enduring framework, including both the high-minded ideals and their insidious practical counterparts. Living with such cross-purposes, the traditional Chinese analyzing their own history have tended to indulge in an oversimplification that stresses the former. The relationship between ideal and real factors, their lack of congruence and their capacity for mutual antagonism, is always hard to analyze in one's own history since it is difficult to achieve an objective point of view. Chinese history offers us a magnificently rich, well-documented, and instructive panorama within which to view this kind of issue.

Antecedents of Legalism

As we look back into the Chou period at the varied Chinese experience with forms and methods of government, we can see several lines of development that contributed to the emergence of Legalism. The importance that Chinese civilization seems always to have attached to analyzing and perfecting the methods of government had established specialization in political techniques long before any Legalist was called that. After the mid-eighth century B.C. especially, as Chou real power declined and that of the states within its nominal hegemony began to increase rapidly, it became abundantly clear that governmental expertise was essential to power. In *The Analects* Confucius repeatedly bemoans the fact that legitimate heads of state merely reign while more competent wielders of illicit power in fact rule. Moreover the states in which this occurred most effectively were those which succeeded best in amassing size and strength and in surviving the turbulent times.

A good example is provided by the state of Ch'i in the seventh century. Ch'i's ruler, Duke Huan (ruled 683–642 B.C.), employed as his chief minister a man called Kuan Chung, the reputed author of the book on statecraft called *The Kuan Tzu*. Kuan Chung died in 645, and on the basis of internal evidence the book could not have been put together until two or three centuries later, but in considerable part it records political thought related to situations and events of the earlier time. Kuan Chung was an expert technician of rulership and statecraft. He invented the institution of the *pa* (pronounced "bah"), or Hegemon, the so-called Lord Protector, a role his patron the duke was first to fill. The concept of the *pa* recognized that, to stabilize the political and military balance among the states making up the Chinese world, it was necessary to maintain the mystique of legitimacy exercised by the powerless Chou kings. This balance was to be maintained by reaffirming the Chou claims to legitimate overlordship and by having a strong man heading a powerful state exercise power in the name of the Chou ruler. Confucius, as might be expected, later criticized many of Kuan Chung's acts, but on the whole was grateful to him for this device, by which the legitimate Chou power was supported, some sense of Chinese unity enhanced, and cultural values protected.

Mencius, disagreeing implicitly with Confucius, denounced the power politics of the Lord Protector system. He developed another political ideal of rule by the true king, the *wang*, whose means were moral force and suasion; he vigorously opposed any legitimation of the sort of military force the *pa* employed. These terms and ideas remained part of the Confucian jargon of politics thereafter. The fact that Kuan Chung remained a symbol about which later Confucians could disagree in itself shows something of the range and vitality of Confucian debate, but also how much more complex the relatively early Confucian political thinking was than later Confucianists have chosen to show.

Kuan Chung had thus, even before the book bearing his name was pieced together, become the symbol of government by a powerful autocrat. He therefore is associated with the tradition out of which

Legalist tendencies emerged. It is interesting to note that his other policies also anticipate Legalism in some important ways. First he openly advocated a government of written laws. In so doing, he avoided any extremes that could not be accommodated to the old Chou traditions and ethical norms. He admired the ancient *t'ien-tse*, or "heavenly norms" embodied in the *Institutes of Chou*, as much as did Confucius, recognizing in them their congruence with human nature. But he thought that such traditional bases of statecraft should be supplemented by clear laws and regulations. Second, Kuan Chung accepted the link between the people's willing support of the ruler and the effectiveness of government, but he nonetheless sought to elevate the ruler to great authority and power so as to strengthen the state. He begins to make the shift of emphasis from the good of the people to the power of the state that eventually was to mark the irreconcilable cleavage between Confucian and Legalist political theory. He went so far as to say that the personal character of the ruler was unimportant, so long as his will was intelligently carried out. Thus the increased power of the state was to go hand in hand with the amoralism that also characterized later Legalism. And the concept of state power as an objective of statecraft also led to a focus on the people as a primary resource. "Cherish the people," an inscription regularly found on Shang and early Chou bronze vessels, exhorts all the king's appointed lords. This ancient recognition of the primary importance of population is idealized in the Confucian tradition to mean that the people's well-being must weigh heavily with rulers. But Kuan Chung's view was less benevolent. Great numbers of people are necessary for a great state, and in power politics people become a material source of political power. Third, Kuan Chung devised techniques to regularize living patterns and control the people more effectively. He experimented with ways of making popular custom uniform; he tried to ensure that the people's energies could be reliably mobilized and at the same time that in their private lives they would not misuse time, energy, or things of utility to the state. Fourth, accompanying these efforts to make the state organizationally and militarily strong, Kuan Chung introduced sweeping innovations in the field of making it rich. He devised state monopoly entrepreneurship in the production and distribution of commodities like iron, salt, and wine. And he attempted to increase the efficiency of production in other areas as well.

Experiments with forms of government, constantly enlarging the role of the ruler and the scope of the state's interests in the people's daily lives, were also carried out in other states. They were not characteristic of those states of which the later Confucians most highly approved, so the record of their activities is not as complete as that of the state of Lu, basically a small and not very important one, whose *Spring and Autumn Annals* (*Ch'un-ch'iu*) form our fullest record of the mid-Chou period. But we can read some brief accounts of the codes of laws used in the states of Cheng and Chin in the seventh, sixth, and fifth centuries. The tradition of using law codes in place of the *Institutes of Chou* (*Chou li, Chou kuan*) apparently was stronger in the states farther to the west and south and in areas where Chou royal court influences and traditions were relatively weak. Something like the later tension between *li* (rites) and law thus seems to have had its antecedents in the varying state practices of mid-Chou times. Only the Confucian filter through which many of the documents later passed and through which the conceptualization of antiquity also later had to pass keeps us from seeing this diversity of practice more clearly.

Another factor is the internal history of the Legalist school. It took form as a coherent position in state theory mostly through the influence of the most successful state minister of that time, Lord Shang, also known as Shang Yang or Kung-sun Yang (d. 338 B.C.). The reward for his success in building up the state of Ch'in was execution by command of his royal master. It was Lord Shang who as chief minister in Ch'in between 361 and 338 launched that state on the successful course toward wealth and power that led directly to the foundation of the Ch'in dynasty in 221 B.C. Whether or not Lord Shang himself wrote the book that bears his name (translated as *The Book of Lord Shang*), it appeared at that time, and it became the first powerful synthetic statement of Legalist doctrines. In it the various traditions of highly specialized statecraft were more or less appropriated by the Legalists, made part of their professional heritage, in the same way that the Confucians appropriated a great deal of document and tradition that antedated their emergence as a philosophical school.

It has been strongly suggested in recent years by H. G. Creel that some of the antecedents of Legalism, notably the school of administrative methods (*shu*) which had as its principal figure Shen Pu-hai (d. 337 B.C.), really had little in common with the spirit and the theory of later Legalism, and that the traditions of the Shen school were more compatible with Confucian attitudes toward government. Yet as interesting as the discovery may prove to be, the Legalist appropriation of Shen Pu-hai served to make his contributions part of that system of ideas. Later Confucianism, utilizing its simplistic framework for the good and the bad, placed him within the camp of the insidious opponent, repudiated *in toto*. So, even if Shen Pu-hai was not a true Legalist, he might as well have been as far as his influence on later Chinese history was concerned.

The antecedents of the formal systematization of Legalist doctrine included the quite extensive discussion of law (*fa*—clear regulations and clear, inescapable penalties) as practiced by Lord Shang; the discussion of administrative methods (*shu*—clear regulations for the bureaucracy and for the functioning of the bureaucratic structure) associated with Shen Pu-hai; and rather more theoretical discussions of a third element usually translated as force or power (*shih*—the implications of position, tendencies latent in relative position, how to bring force to bear in situations of competing power). This last area of Legalist theory is associated with a thinker called Shen Tao (d. ca. 275 B.C.). The great synthesis of these theories and practices was accomplished by Han Fei or Han Fei Tzu, the ex-Confucian and former student of Hsün Tzu. This misguided genius is one of the most impressive political thinkers of all time. A prince of the ducal house of Han who had offered his services and his theories to the state of Ch'in because Legalist approaches were being rigorously applied there, Han Fei was too dangerous a resource to be allowed to wander free and perhaps fall into the service of some rival state. So the Ch'in king and his chief minister arranged to force suicide upon him.

That chief minister to the king in Ch'in was Li Ssu, Han Fei's fellow student at the feet of Hsün Tzu. No theoretician of government, but the supreme practitioner of Legalist methods, Li Ssu was the master builder of the Chinese empire. And the Ch'in king, his royal employer, was the monster of Chinese history. He first occupied the imperial mansion, built to Legalist designs, on foundations laid down a century earlier by Lord Shang, held together (briefly to be sure) with the cynical essence of political craft distilled by Han Fei.

Legalism is not a movement in philosophy. It is not concerned with truth. It is not reflective thinking on the great individual and social problems of life. It does not seek the general principles under which all facts can be explained. It is a system of methods and principles for the operation of the state, and even the state is given only the barest of ideological foundations. Legalists were content to justify their system by the single comment: "It works." They believed in the state purely for its own sake, but they never explained why. Han Fei, incongruous as it may seem (and certainly is), hints that he felt the all-powerful ruler of the totally efficient state fulfilled some Taoist principle of "doing nothing, yet accomplishing everything"; but even such tenuous links to outraged philosophy are difficult to establish. What further philosophical foundations Legalism had were drawn from subtle and perceptive observations of social-psychological phenomena. It was a system for manipulating human behavior, for making people forgo their natural individual interests in the service of the state. Legalism had no speculative interest in the inapplicable, like cosmology and metaphysics, and it could abandon logic, since it was based on stronger forces than reason. Ethics was irrelevant, yet the Legalist state was happy to see that people's lives could be normalized and made predictable by adherence to codes of behavior, as long as these did not interfere with state interests or diminish the sovereign's range of action.

How could such a system of ideas draw the best minds of an age to its service? Legalists shared one great overriding concern with the other schools of thought: How to achieve stability in an age of turmoil. This quite valid cause drew to it men anxious to perfect political instruments without reference to morals, traditions, and philosophical subtleties. It produced a corpus of political writings without parallel for breadth and analytical perceptiveness. It failed ultimately when practiced on a large scale, perhaps because of its philosophical aridity. Its understanding of human nature was necessarily cynical and limited by that fact in practical application. For even this most thoroughgoing and perceptive distillation of the means to manipulate human beings through enticement and intimidation failed as a total system of controlled human behavior: It was too rational, too self-enclosed, to comprehend—let alone manipulate—all the mysteries of the human heart. Legalism provided the actual means of organizing the vast machinery of Chinese government and of uniting the nation into a coherent, governable whole to a point only a frightening shade short of success. That success was achieved in the next dynasty, when, following the brief Ch'in interlude, some of the Legalist essentials were modified and combined with a more perceptive, if less neat, philosophy of human nature, that is, the Confucian tradition as it then existed. Before

examining the form that that unlikely amalgam was to assume, some
further events of Ch'in history demand brief attention.

Legalism in Action

King Cheng of Ch'in has been made a monster in Chinese history.
That, we might well observe, is a curious way for a civilization's historians to treat the man who undoubtedly would be the great hero of
another national history. The unification of China that King Cheng
accomplished was something like winning a race among the five or six
remaining states, swollen survivors of the multistate system of mid-
Chou and earlier times. Throughout the Warring States period there
was a growing expectation—and desire—that a great king would
emerge in one of the states. By the force of his overwhelming virtue
(as Mencius anticipated the event) or overwhelming might (as the
Legalists in Ch'in planned it) or a faltering combination of the two (as
most of the other states with less than single-minded determination
attempted it), this new superking would "restore" political unity, impose peace, and commence a great new age. Would it be the state of
Ch'i in the Northeast, heir alike to Kuan Chung's policies and to the
Chou traditions maintained in its centers of ancient learning? Or
would it be Ch'u, the great state of the central Yangtze valley in the
South, heir to the diverse cultural strands of that frontier region but
waxing mightily in importance in the power relations of the Chinese
heartland? Or, Heaven forbid, would it be the ruthless state of Ch'in
on the northwest frontier? Or could an alliance of anti-Ch'in states be
formed to forestall the holocaust?

For a century the Chinese observed the major actors and their
maneuvers. In each generation the cleverest and most ambitious men
examined the probabilities, philosophized about the moral implications, chose sides, offered their military skills and their stratagems,
their hearts and their tongues. The burgeoning new class of business-
men made fortunes in strategic goods and in speculation. Military
chiefs were constantly busy as the art of war was totally reconstituted
to take into account mass conscript armies, multifaceted technological
advance, and new attitudes toward war. And the common people
found in the turbulent social scene outlets for talent and new freedom
of choice in designing their lives, but even more, the miseries of

incessant warfare. The close of the long Chou era is one of the great watersheds of Chinese history.

In the hindsight of history it is hard to see how any mid-third-century B.C. observer could have mistaken the sure signs of eventual Ch'in victory. King Cheng came to the throne as a boy in 246 B.C., and he reigned for thirty-six years. Throughout that long reign he was served in turn by two vigorous and brilliant chief ministers. Statist policies had long been consistently maintained and efficiently implemented. The work of Lord Shang a century earlier had borne fruit in organization, efficiency, wealth, and great military power. In addition to first-rate assistance in civil administration, King Cheng was served by great generals, among them Meng T'ien, who defended the Central Asian frontier and built there the Great Wall of China. Perceptive political analysts like Han Fei saw the Ch'in star rising and volunteered service as did Li Ssu, the ambitious operator. But most Chinese of the time were probably far too emotionally involved to possess such detached and calculating power of observation.

King Cheng himself is a figure so wrapped in partisan historiography that it is difficult to assess his personal role in the great events. He may have had little to contribute as a personality other than to play the role of the symbolic head of state. We know that he was an enormously active man, a demon for work by day and reputedly an insatiable lover by night, but it is entirely possible that his frenetic energies were expended in ways quite incidental to the success of the great plot. In any event the Ch'in machine worked perfectly to produce that success, and in the twenty-sixth year of his reign King Cheng saw the military sweep of the remaining rival states accomplished. The states to the west and the center were exterminated in the years following 230 B.C. Ch'u was annihilated in 224 to 223; Yen and Tai in the north fell in 222; and in 221 Ch'i, the last holdout, was vanquished. The world was his.

In that year King Cheng, acting on the advice of his ministers, declared himself the "First August Supreme Ruler" (*Shih huang ti*) of the world, by which he meant the civilized central "Chinese" regions of the world as then known to East Asians. The title he adopted was new, an arrogant creation far beyond the pretensions of the Chou kings and all the rulers of antiquity. Yet "August Supreme Ruler" (*huang ti*) remained the title taken by all bearers of the Mandate throughout all successive dynasties until 1911 and by two or three pretenders since then. The arrogance of the innovator became the minimal claim of his successors. And this was true not only of vain titles, but more importantly, of the basic forms and instruments created within his reign to rule over the vast state that had just been born.

We usually translate his self-appointed new title as simply "emperor," and call him, as he numbered himself, the First Emperor (*Shih Huang Ti*). For that reason the unified Chinese state that came into being at that moment in history is usually called the Chinese empire to contrast it with the dynastic periods of the Chou and earlier kingdoms. This political title remained until the Republican Revolution in 1911. The Chou had been nominally suzerains over the states that properly started out as dukedoms and marquisates (to use another set of familiar analogies) until they raised themselves to "kingdoms" in the Warring States period. But whether words like "kingdom" and "empire" should be used in Chinese history is open to some question.

In the West "empire" has usually meant a kingdom expanded by conquest to rule over additional territories whose people were distinct in history, language, and culture; that was the distinction between the English kingdom and the British empire, between the kingdoms of medieval Europe and the Holy Roman Empire. Yet even in these examples, usage differs from its earlier source, the Roman *imperium* whose *imperator* was essentially a military commander. The analogies are not precise, but the usage is fixed in all these cases. Our justification, perhaps an adequate one, for calling China an empire after 221 B.C. is that its rulers from that time onward considered themselves raised in dignity above the *wang* of yore (whom we have called "kings"), and in fact they possessed much greater power in a state that was henceforth to be centrally administered in direct response to their authority. The important difference to remember is that the Chinese emperors, with but few exceptions, did not attempt to extend their direct rule over peoples beyond the pale of their culture and language, nor did the assumption of the new title signify to them *that* difference from their earlier national history. Within the area to which their government's uniform administration applied, essential cultural unity had always existed. Their administration depended on the unity of that cultural base. Even the differences between local dialects and regional sublanguages, thanks to the characteristics of the Chinese script, were diluted by complete linguistic unity on the level of written

language. By all other cultural tests, including that of their own awareness of their "Chinese" distinctiveness and cultural centrality as a
community in the world, the Chinese were one people. National political unity, achieved belatedly in 221 B.C., simply expressed a preexisting
and continuously maintained fact of their history.

"Imperial China" applied to Ch'in and Han and later dynasties
does not designate an era in which Chinese suzerainty was extended
over non-Chinese peoples, nor of any intent to extend Chinese suzerainty beyond its traditional limits.* The use of the terms "Chinese
empire" and "Imperial China," then, starting with the Ch'in unification in 221 B.C., indicates a new era in the structure and the manner
of domestic politics and designates in a general way the political life
of China in the two millennia of that era; it has no particular implications for China's relations with non-Chinese peoples beyond her bor-
ders.

We really know little about the First Emperor, the man who gets
so little credit from the Chinese historians for his part in these great
events. He apparently was something less than a monster, and he
certainly was less than the perfect Legalist sovereign who "does nothing but accomplishes everything." He appears to have been at the very
least a shrewd, hard-working, power-crazy eccentric, a man who traveled restlessly throughout his realm, who built walls and palaces and
great roadways indefatigably, who credulously sought the aid of spirits
and gods, and who strove to uncover the secret of immortality. The
regime he headed was marked by trickery, brute force, and harsh law,
which earned him the undying hatred of Chinese in all walks of life
throughout his reign, and also stirred a resentment against him virtually without equal in all of Chinese history. Only in the twentieth
century have radically revisionist historians been able to argue that for
all his faults he accomplished great things and made imperishable
contributions to his country's history. Yet they still find more to

---

* An important exception, seemingly, is the imperialism of the Manchu dynasty that
ruled China from 1644 to 1911, and that aggressively extended its rule, in the name
of the Chinese empire of which it had become the master, into Central Asia and
Tibet; but even under those rather exceptional and perhaps non-Chinese circumstances, special forms of attenuated administration were adopted for areas beyond the
range of Chinese culture, and the hand of the imperial master on those regions was
rather light.

criticize than to praise. But was he in fact more "monstrous" than a Caesar or a Napoleon?

The point is obvious, but it is worth remembering: He was judged by his own countrymen according to their cultural values, and these provided quite different standards from those by which the heroic accomplishers of other civilizations have been judged. The judgments themselves tell us much about the men in question, but even more about the civilizations.

The First Emperor, who had occupied a hundred splendid palaces and countless beds, died on the road among his imperial entourage during one of his unending "tours of inspection." He died in the year 210, a man in his early fifties, of some sudden digestive illness, in fact probably induced by exhaustion—an odd irony for the ruler who theoretically was supposed to "accomplish everything while doing nothing." The construction of his grandiose tomb in the outskirts of his capital, to the east of modern Sian (Xi'an) had been underway for many years. He was buried in its underground palace, topped by an artificially heaped-up mountain, guarded on all sides by regiments of terra-cotta warriors. The accidental discovery in 1974 of the outer fringes of the tomb complex exposed over seven thousand life-size sculptures of warriors and horses, equipped with chariots and bronze weapons—the most important archeological discovery of recent decades. It bears witness to the might of the Ch'in state and the vast scope of the First Emperor's measures. His burial chamber eventually will be explored, and its contents may help us to reassess this man and his age. His reign proved to be of greatest consequence for all subsequent history, although he lived only a dozen years after completing the unification in 221 B.C.

Without his presence at the head of it all, the Legalist machinery of state collapsed, thereby dramatically either denying the Legalist character of his state or contradicting completely all the theory of Legalism. For in theory the Legalist state should function perfectly by the working of its laws; any person should serve as well as any other in the role of supreme ruler. The remaining few years of his "everlasting" dynasty are a parody of the awesome Ch'in rise to power. Bumbling courtiers, concerned with petty self-interest, manipulated the succession, destroyed an able legitimate heir, brought a simpleton to the throne as Second August Supreme Ruler, and did away with Li Ssu, the skilled operator of the machinery of state.

Once the dynasty lost its central leadership and its carefully implemented momentum, its claims to Legalist invincibility were open sham. Revolt arose in all the provinces, and the ensuing civil war was between rival successors, not between the Ch'in state and its internal enemies. In a brief but destructive period of general war from 209 until 202 B.C., the dynasty of Ch'in vanished, but its centralized empire remained as the prize to be captured intact by a new bearer of the Mandate. In that civil war, the opposing lines were eventually drawn on the issues of aristocratic restoration of the pre-Ch'in status quo versus a populist rebellion looking rather vaguely toward some kind of post-Ch'in new world. The latter side, by no particular inevitability of history, happened to win, and the Han dynasty succeeded the Ch'in to endure for four hundred years and to give the imperial era its true foundation—in the retrospective view of Chinese civilization.

Bibliography

GENERAL

*Chan, Wing-tsit. A Source Book in Chinese Philosophy. Princeton, N.J.: Princeton University Press, 1963. Meticulous translations; insightful comment; the indispensable handbook for students of Chinese thought from the beginnings to the present.

*Hsiao, Kung-chuan. A History of Chinese Political Thought, Volume 1, From the Beginnings to the Sixth Century A.D. Translated into English by F. W. Mote. Princeton, N.J.: Princeton University Press, 1979. Much Chinese philosophy developed within the focus of political thought, hence the centrality of this work to the study of China's early intellectual history.

Schwarz, Benjamin I. The World of Thought in Ancient China. Cambridge, Mass.: Belknap Press of Harvard University Press, 1985. Stimulating reflections on Chinese philosophical concerns by a scholar whose profound cultivation in Western intellectual traditions gives this work its special character.

CHAPTER 1:   THE HISTORICAL BEGINNINGS

Chang, Kwang-chih. The Archeology of Ancient China. 4th ed. New Haven, Conn.: Yale University Press, 1986.

Cheng, Te-k'un. Archeology in China. Vol. 1, Prehistoric China. Supplement to Vol. 1, New Light on Prehistoric China. Vol. 2, Shang China. Vol. 3, Chou China. Toronto: University of Toronto Press, 1961–1964.

Creel, H. G. The Birth of China: A Survey of the Formative Period of Chinese Civilization. 1936. Reprint. New York: Ungar, 1954.

Cressey, George B. The Land of the Five Hundred Million: A Geography of China. New York: McGraw-Hill, 1955.

Ho, P. T. "The Loess and the Origin of Chinese Agriculture." American Historical Review 75 (October 1969): 1–36.

---

*Available in paperback.

*Keightley, David N. *The Origins of Chinese Civilization.* Berkeley, Calif.: University of California Press, 1983.

Li, Chi. *The Beginnings of Chinese Civilization.* Seattle, Wash.: University of Washington Press, 1957.

Schafer, Edward H. *Ancient China.* New York: Time-Life Books, 1967.

*Watson, William. *Early Civilization in China.* New York: McGraw-Hill, 1966.

CHAPTER 2:   THE BEGINNINGS OF A WORLD VIEW

*Bloom, Allan. *The Closing of the American Mind.* New York: Simon & Schuster, 1987.

*Bodde, Derk. "Myths of Ancient China." In *Mythologies of the Ancient World,* edited by S. N. Kramer. New York: Doubleday Anchor Books, 1961.

Bradie, Michael. "Recent Developments in the Physics of Time and General Cosmology." *Journal of Chinese Philosophy* 12 (December 1985): 370–95. Not specifically about China, but useful for comparisons here.

*Ho, Pen Yoke. *Li, Qi and Shu: An Introduction to Science and Civilization in China.* HongKong: University of HongKong Press, 1985. An introduction to Needham (below), focusing on the fundamental concepts of mathematics, astronomy, and alchemy in early China.

I Ching, or Book of Changes. Translated into English by Cary F. Baynes from the German translation of Richard Wilhelm. Foreword by Carl Jung. Prefaces by Richard and Hellmut Wilhelm. Bollingen Series, vol. 19. Princeton, N.J.: Princeton University Press, 1967.

Legge, James, trans. *The Chinese Classics.* 5 vols. Reprint. HongKong: University of HongKong Press, 1960.

Needham, Joseph, and Wang Ling. *Science and Civilization in China.* 16 vols. to date. Cambridge: Cambridge University Press, 1954–. See especially Vol. 2.

Schafer, Edward H. "The Idea of Created Nature in T'ang Literature." *Philosophy East and West* 15 (April 1965): 153–160.

Sivin, Nathan. "Chinese Conceptions of Time." *The Earlham Review* 1 (Fall 1966): 83–92.

*Available in paperback.

*Wilhelm, Hellmut. *Change: Eight Lectures on the I Ching.* Translated by Cary F. Baynes. Bollingen Series, vol. 62. Princeton, N.J.: Princeton University Press, 1960.

CHAPTER 3:   EARLY CONFUCIANISM

*Creel, H. G. *Confucius and the Chinese Way.* New York: Harper, 1960.

Hsiao, K.C. *A History of Chinese Political Thought.* English Edition. Princeton, N.J.: Princeton University Press, 1979.

*Lau, D.C. *The Analects.* London: Penguin, 1979.

*Lau, D.C. *Mencius.* London: Penguin, 1970.

Legge, James, trans. *The Chinese Classics.* 5 vols. Reprint. HongKong: University of HongKong Press, 1960.

Richards, I. A. *Mencius on the Mind.* London: Kegan Paul, 1932.

*Tu, Wei-ming. *Centrality and Commonality: An Essay on Chung-yung.* Honolulu, Hawaii: University Press of Hawaii, 1976.

*Tu, Wei-ming. *Confucian Thought: Selfhood as Creative Transformation.* Albany, N.Y.: State University Press of New York, 1985.

Waley, Arthur, trans. *The Analects of Confucius.* London: Allen and Unwin, 1938.

*Waley, Arthur. *Three Ways of Thought in Ancient China.* Reprint. Garden City, N.Y.: Doubleday Anchor Books, 1956.

*Watson, Burton, trans. *Hsün Tzu: Basic Writings.* New York: Columbia University Press, 1963.

CHAPTER 4:   EARLY TAOISM

A. Translations of the *Tao Te Ching:*

*Chan, W. T. *The Way of Lao Tzu.* New York: Macmillan, 1963.

Duyvendak, J. J. L. *Tao Te Ching: The Book of the Way and Its Virtue.* London: John Murray, 1954.

*Lau, D. C. *Tao Te Ching.* London: Penguin, 1963.

*Lau, D. C. *Tao Te Ching.* HongKong: Chinese University Press, 1982. Includes translation based on the Ma-wang-tui silk manuscript and comparisons with the traditional Wang Pi version.

---

*Available in paperback.

*Lin, Paul J. A *Translation of Lao Tzu's Tao Te Ching and Wang Pi's Commentary.* Center for Chinese Studies, Ann Arbor, Mich.: University of Michigan Press, 1977. Translates the most important of the early commentaries and compares the Ma-wang-tui text.

Lin Yutang. *The Wisdom of Laotse.* New York: Modern Library, 1948.

*Waley, Arthur. *The Way and Its Power: A Study of the Tao Te Ching and Its Place in Chinese Thought.* Reprint. New York: Grove Press, 1958.

B. Translations of the *Chuang Tzu:*

Fung, Yu-lan. *Chuang Tzu.* Reprint. New York: Paragon, 1964.

*Waley, Arthur. *Three Ways of Thought in Ancient China.* Garden City, N.Y.: Doubleday Anchor Books, 1956.

*Watson, Burton, trans. *The Complete Works of Chuang Tzu.* New York: Columbia University Press, 1968.

*————. *Chuang Tzu: Basic Writings.* New York: Columbia University Press, 1964.

C. Other Works:

Chang, Chung-yuan. *Creativity and Taoism.* New York: Julian Press, 1963.

Creel, Herrlee G. "On the Opening Words of the *Lao-tzu.*" *Journal of Chinese Philosophy* 10 (December 1983): 299–329. Learned discussion of problems in Lao Tzu and Taoism generally.

*Kaltenmark, Max. *Lao Tzu and Taoism.* Translated by Roger Greaves. Stanford, Calif.: Stanford University Press, 1969.

*Welch, Holmes. *The Parting of the Way: Lao Tzu and the Taoist Movement.* Boston: Beacon Press, 1957.

CHAPTER 5:   MO TZU: HIS PHILOSOPHICAL IDEAS

Mei, Y. P., trans. *The Ethical and Political Works of Motse.* London: Probsthain, 1929.

Mei, Y. P. *Motse, the Neglected Rival of Confucius.* London: Probsthain, 1934.

*Waley, Arthur. *Three Ways of Thought in Ancient China.* Reprint. Garden City, N.Y.: Doubleday Anchor Books, 1956.

*Available in paperback.

*Watson, Burton, trans. *Mo Tzu: The Basic Writings.* New York: Columbia University Press, 1963.

CHAPTER 6:   THE PROBLEM OF KNOWLEDGE

Chao, Y. R. *Aspects of Chinese Socio-Linguistics.* Edited by A. S. Dil. Stanford, Calif.: Stanford University Press, 1976. Especially section 3, "Philosophical Perspectives." This analyzes problems of logic in modern Chinese, but has implications for similar issues in classical Chinese.

Ch'eng, Chung-ying. "Inquiries into Classical Chinese Logic." *Philosophy East and West* 15 (July and October 1965): 195–216.

Chmielewski, Januz. "Notes on Early Chinese Logic." *Rocznik Orientalistyczny* 26–32 (eight installments 1962–1969).

Eberhard, Wolfram. Review of *Science and Civilization in China,* Volume 1. *Journal of Asian Studies* 19 (November 1959).

Graham, A. C. "The Logic of the Mohist *Hsiao-ch'ü.*" *T'oung Pao* 51 (1964): 1–54.

————. "The Place of Reason in the Chinese Philosophical Tradition." In R. Dawson, *The Legacy of China.* Oxford: Clarendon Press, 1964.

————. *Later Mohist Logic, Ethics and Science.* HongKong: Chinese University Press, 1978. The summation of this eminent expert's work on Mohist ways of thinking.

Hanson, Chad. *Language and Logic in Ancient China.* Ann Arbor, Mich.: University of Michigan Press, 1983.

————. "Chinese Language, Chinese Philosophy, and 'Truth.'" *Journal of Asian Studies* 44 (May 1985): 491–519. A specialist in linguistic philosophy, Hanson in these two works offers strikingly different analyses of issues in early Chinese thought.

Hu, Shih. *The Development of the Logical Method in Ancient China.* Reprint. New York: Paragon, 1963.

Mei, Y. P. "Some Observations on the Problem of Knowledge Among the Ancient Chinese Logicians." *Tsing Hua Journal of Chinese Studies* 1 (1956): 114–121.

Shih, Vincent Y. C. "Hsün Tzu's Positivism." *Tsing Hua Journal of Chinese Studies* 4 (1964).

*Available in paperback.

CHAPTER 7:   THE CREATION OF THE CHINESE EMPIRE

Bodde, Derk. *China's First Unifier: A Study of the Ch'in Dynasty as Seen in the Life of Li Ssu, 280?–208 B.C.* Leiden: E. J. Brill, 1938.

———, trans. *Statesman, Patriot and General in Ancient China.* New Haven, Conn.: American Oriental Society, 1940.

Creel, Herrlee G. *The Origins of Statecraft in China.* Vol. 1, *The Western Chou Empire.* Chicago: University of Chicago Press, 1970.

———. *Shen Pu-hai, A Chinese Political Philosopher of the Fourth Century B.C.* Chicago: University of Chicago Press, 1974. These learned works question traditional explanations of Legalism.

Duyvendak, J. J. L., trans. *The Book of Lord Shang.* London: Probsthain, 1928.

*Hsü Cho-yin. *Ancient China in Transition.* Stanford, Calif.: Stanford University Press, 1965.

*Kierman, Frank A., Jr. *Four Warring States Biographies.* Wiesbaden, Germany: Otto Harrassowitz, 1962.

Li, Yu-ning, ed. *The First Emperor of China: The Politics of Historiography.* White Plains, N.Y.: International Arts and Sciences Press, 1975. Translations of traditional sources and recent scholarship, focusing on Communist Chinese interpretations of the founding of the Chinese empire.

———. *Shang Yang's Reforms and State Control in China.* White Plains, N. Y.: M. E. Sharpe, 1977. Similar to the preceding, focused on the early Legalist phase of the state of Ch'in.

Rickett, W. Allyn. *Guanzi: Political, Economic and Philosophical Essays from Early China—A Study and Translation.* Vol. 1. Princeton, N.J.: Princeton University Press, 1985.

Walker, Richard L. *The Multi-State System of Ancient China.* Hamden, Conn.: Shoe String Press, 1953.

Watson, Burton, trans. *Records of the Grand Historian of China.* Translated from the *Shih Chi* of Ssu-ma Ch'ien. 2 vols. New York: Columbia University Press, 1961.

*———, trans. *Han Fei Tzu: Basic Writings.* New York: Columbia University Press, 1964.

*Available in paperback.

Chronology of
Early Chinese
Schools of Thought

Chronology

	CONFUCIAN SCHOOL	TAOIST SCHOOL	OTHER INDIVIDUALS AND SCHOOLS	LEGALIST SCHOOL
600 B.C.				
550 B.C.	Confucius 551–479	Lao Tzu?		Tzu-ch'an's Law Code 543
500 B.C.		The compiling of the *Tao Te Ching*?		
475 B.C.?			Mo Tzu ca. 479–438	
450 B.C.	The compiling of *The Doctrine of the Mean* and *The Great Learning*			Lord Shang ?–388

Ch'un-Ch'iu Period

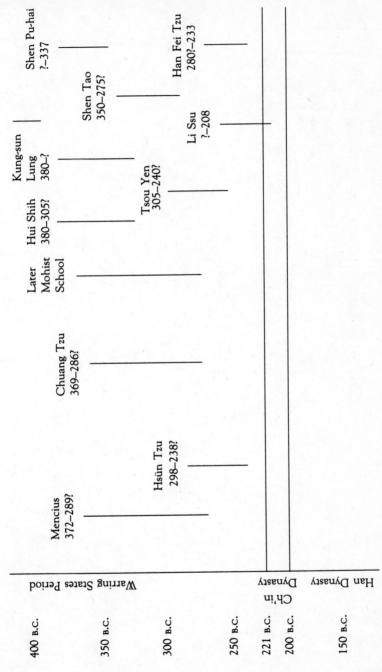

Mencius
372–289?

Hsün Tzu
298–238?

Chuang Tzu
369–286?

Later
Mohist
School

Hui Shih
380–305?

Kung-sun
Lung
380–?

Tsou Yen
305–240?

Shen Tao
350–275?

Shen Pu-hai
?–337

Li Ssu
?–208

Han Fei Tzu
280?–233

Warring States Period

Ch'in
Dynasty

Han Dynasty

400 B.C.

350 B.C.

300 B.C.

250 B.C.

221 B.C.

200 B.C.

150 B.C.

Index

About the Author

Frederick W. Mote is Professor emeritus at Princeton University, where he taught from 1956 to 1987. He received his B.A. in Chinese History from the University of Nanking (China) and his M.A. and Ph.D. in Chinese History from the University of Washington (Seattle). Widely published in scholarly journals, Professor Mote is also the author of *The Poet Kao Ch'i*; co-editor and author of chapters in Volumes VI, VII, VIII of the *Cambridge History of China*; and the translator of *History of Chinese Political Thought* by K. C. Hsiao. Professor Mote was the recipient of a Guggenheim fellowship in 1968 and 1987.

A Note on the Type

The text of this book has been set in Goudy Old Style, one of the more than 100 type faces designed by Frederic William Goudy (1865–1947). Although Goudy began his career as a bookkeeper, he was so inspired by the appearance of several newly published books from the Kelmscott Press that he devoted the remainder of his life to typography in an attempt to bring a better understanding of the movement led by William Morris to the printers of the United States.

Produced in 1914, Goudy Old Style reflects the absorption of a generation of designers with things "ancient." Its smooth, even color combined with its generous curves and ample cut marks it as one of Goudy's finest achievements.